THE AMERICAN SAILING ASSOCIATION'S

CRUISING CATAMARANS MADE EASY

THE OFFICIAL MANUAL OF THE AMERICAN SAILING ASSOCIATION'S CRUISING CATAMARAN STANDARD (ASA114)

Produced for ASA by

Amanda Lunn Design and Publishing

www.amandalunnpublishing.com

proofreader Jo Weeks

indexer Penelope Kent

First published by American Sailing Association in 2016

American Sailing Association
5301 Beethoven Street, Suite #265
Los Angeles, CA 90066

ISBN 978-0-9821025-4-1

Printed in the U.S.

Learning to sail is just the beginning.

Become a member today and make your sailing lifestyle richer. Let's sail off together on an incredibly fun ASA flotilla, take a bareboating course, or let ASA's FindMyCharter.com help you find the charter of your dreams. Scan here (or visit www.asa.com) for more information on all the great benefits that ASA membership has to offer.

www.asa.com

CONTENTS

THE AMERICAN SAILING ASSOCIATION

The American Sailing Association was founded in 1983 with a simply stated mission: to teach people to sail safely and confidently. To achieve that goal, the ASA set out to establish standards against which to measure a sailor's level of knowledge and skill, the first such unified standards in the USA to apply to sailors in keelboats.

After studying programs offered in other countries, the founders of the ASA selected the Canadian Yachting Association's (CYA) "Learn to Cruise" program and licensed it for use in the US. With this strong heritage behind it, the ASA has continually improved and expanded its educational system by drawing on valuable input from the ASA school network.

Today, the ASA is an association of sailing schools, charter companies, professional sailing instructors, and sailors, with over 300 affiliated sailing schools located throughout the United States, as well as in Europe, Japan, Central America, Taiwan, China, and other Far Eastern countries. These accredited schools offer ASA certification to individuals who meet the requirements for a given level.

This book, *Cruising Catamarans Made Easy*, is the textbook for the Cruising Catamaran Standard, which builds on the first three primary levels of student certification within the ASA keelboat progression: Basic Keelboat Sailing, Basic Coastal Cruising, and Bareboat Cruising. Students who successfully complete both the written and practical on-water exams for this level have proven that they have acquired the special knowledge that will enable them to act as skipper and crew of an auxiliary-powered sailing cruising catamaran within the same general parameters as laid out in the Bareboat Cruising standard for keelboats.

Whether your goal is to charter a boat in Tahiti or to crew confidently on a short weekend sail, the ASA's sailing-education system will guide you as you learn the theory behind sailing, practice the skills needed to handle a sailboat, and build the foundation of knowledge that will enable you to navigate a vessel safely and within the law.

By establishing national standards for sailing education, the ASA has provided a way for more people to take part in the sport safely, with the proper training and respect for their responsibilities as boaters, ensuring that sailing will be safer, smarter, and more fun for everybody.

For more information please visit our website at www.asa.com.

Charlie Nobles
ASA EXECUTIVE DIRECTOR

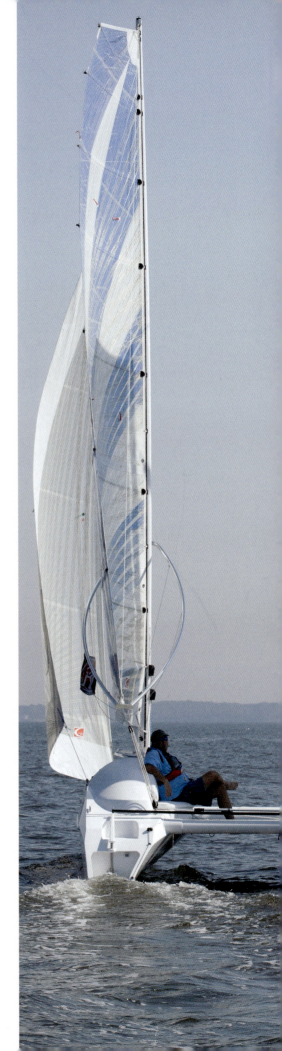

THE AIM OF THIS BOOK

It is the aim of this book to provide you with the knowledge required to act as skipper and crew of an auxiliary-powered cruising catamaran of approximately 30 to 45 feet in length during a multi-day liveaboard cruise upon inland or coastal waters in moderate to heavy winds and sea conditions.

Cruising catamarans continue to grow in popularity, partially because of their ability to provide a very comfortable environment while offering a stable platform and plenty of room and privacy for everybody. This makes them ideal vacation yachts for you and your family or a group of friends. They also seem to be available for charter almost everywhere in the world you would want to sail.

While the basic principles of sailing stand true, from the smallest boat to the biggest, there are big differences in the way these multihulled boats handle, both under sail and under power. Moreover, cruising catamarans not only have more volume and more freeboard than monohulls, they are usually propelled by two engines and also have twice as many systems to monitor.

The context of this book builds upon your successful completion of all of the prerequisites, ASA's 101 (Basic Keelboat Sailing), 103 (Basic Coastal Cruising), and 104 (Bareboat Cruising) Standards.

While this book is an excellent teaching tool for sailors who want to learn on their own, no text can substitute for the personal insights and individual attention an ASA instructor can provide.

Anyone interested in learning how to sail using the American Sailing Association system should begin with ASA101 *Sailing Made Easy*.

Lenny Shabes
ASA CHAIRMAN OF THE BOARD

CONTRIBUTORS

ASA would like to acknowledge the contributions of the writers and editors who made this book possible.

WRITERS

Andy Batchelor was born in Weymouth, England, the venue for the 2012 London Olympics sailing events. On retiring from the Royal Air Force in 2002 as a wing commander, Andy decided to embark on a new career in sailing after meeting his future wife, Lisa Frailey, in Italy. Together they launched Sail Solomons School and Charters, which has since received ASA's "Outstanding School" five times. Andy, a USCG Captain and ASA Instructor Evaluator, has received ASA's "Outstanding Instructor" award seven times and his vast experience aboard monohulls and multihulls was invaluable in the co-writing of this book.

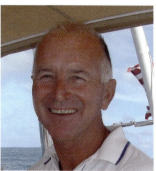

Lisa Batchelor Frailey was dunked into the Chesapeake Bay as a baby and marinized for life. She retired from the US Navy as a captain in 2006, after a career as navigator, meteorologist, and oceanographer that allowed her to cruise and race on many exotic seas — she met her husband, Andy Batchelor, at a regatta in the Bay of Napoli. In 2014, she and Andy launched Kinetic Sailing to expand the scope of their charter, instruction, and consulting activities. Lisa is a USCG Captain, ocean passagemaker, marine consultant, charter broker, flotilla leader, and a five-time recipient of ASA's "Outstanding Instructor" award. She has written about her passion — sailing — in many nautical publications.

EDITORS

Jeremy McGeary left England on an ebb tide in 1970 and rode it through a five-year spell in the Caribbean charter trade before fetching up in the US, where he turned his attention to designing sailboats and writing for sailing magazines. After several years in the editorial department at *Cruising World* magazine, he became Senior Editor at *Good Old Boat* magazine, where he helps sailors share their fondness for maintaining, restoring, and seeking adventure in their older fiberglass sailboats.

Peter Isler is one of America's best known sailors both on and off the water. Since being named Collegiate Sailor of the Year while at Yale University, he has been part of five America's Cup campaigns, winning it twice (once on a catamaran) as navigator aboard Dennis Conner's *Stars & Stripes* and covering it five times on television. He has written several books, including Peter Isler's *Little Blue Book of Sailing Secrets*, and co-authored the best-selling *Sailing for Dummies*. Still active as a professional sailor, Peter is also a popular motivational speaker for corporate audiences. As a director of ASA since 1983, he has devoted a great deal of his time to bringing fresh faces into sailing.

Lenny Shabes is the founder of the American Sailing Association and is currently the Chairman of the Board. His first sailing experience was maneuvering a model boat on a lake in Central Park at age 8. Hooked for life, he has since raced and cruised around the world. He has been a boat broker, sailing instructor, and charter-boat captain. He has owned a sailing school and a charter company and has generally been involved in the marine industry for over 35 years. He and his wife, Cindy, currently own a J/100 that they race and day sail out of Marina del Rey, California.

Charles "Charly" Devanneaux has been a sailor all his life. As a young man, he raced 18-foot sport cats and competed in many top-level regattas and singlehanded races in Europe. He has also raced three times to Hawaii doublehanded in the Transpac and Pacific Cup. He has twice crossed the Atlantic on a catamaran and can count 20,000 miles sailing catamarans on every sea in the world. Charly lives in Los Angeles, where he has one of the largest dealerships for Lagoon Catamarans in America. His personal boat, a Lagoon 450, is his fourth cruising catamaran. Charly was involved in the creation of the Beneteau ASA First 22, the first boat ever made specifically for ASA sailing schools.

photography

Billy Black has been called an artist with a camera. He started his career in photography in the New York fashion industry but quickly discovered that he preferred traveling to capture the magic of the light and the spirit of the people in new places. He sailed his Ericson 39 into Newport for the start of the 1986 BOC Challenge and moved to Rhode Island in 1991. Billy works out of his office in Portsmouth, Rhode Island, with his wife, Joyce, and assistant, Jennifer Tinkoff. He specializes in publicity work for all kinds of boats but also enjoys adventure-sailing photography.

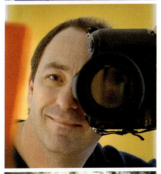

Nicolas Claris was born in an old fishing neighborhood close to Cannes on the French Riviera. He grew up loving the sea and worked as a boatbuilder and professional skipper and has sailed the world over, but photography became his vocation in 1999 and he began shooting for yacht builders, architects, and designers. His passion for boats and sailing were the reason yachts became such a large portion of his portfolio, but he has also focused on architecture and nature in all its details. Nicolas lives by his convictions, and believes the photographer's blue note is in the dying glow of the sunset.

artwork

Peter Bull has worked as a freelance illustrator for over 25 years. His studio has produced illustrations for sailing manuals for many years. Peter works from his studio (Peter Bull Art Studio) based at his home in Wadhurst, East Sussex, England, with illustrators and designers creating work for the publishing and advertising industries worldwide.

ACKNOWLEDGEMENTS

ASA is also deeply grateful to the following people who have contributed their knowledge, guidance, and time to the realization of *Cruising Catamarans Made Easy*: **Cynthia Shabes** President, **Charlie Nobles** Executive Director, **Brenda Wempner** Program Development

Thanks also to **Lagoon America** for providing a Lagoon 39 for photography in Annapolis, Maryland, and to Charly Devanneaux for sharing his skill, knowledge, and patience while skippering it.

To augment Billy Black's impressive portfolio of stock and assignment images, ASA reached out to the broad community of catamaran designers, builders, and photographers. Credits for those images appear on page 90.

FOREWORD

You've made a great decision to learn how to sail and cruise in a catamaran. Welcome to my world and get ready for some good times! You are about to embark on a fun and exciting journey filled with new and challenging adventures.

I fell in love with going fast on catamarans at an early age and helped popularize big catamaran racing in the U.S. It's personally very rewarding to see the world of sailing finally embrace the catamaran and cats become the boat of choice for cruising sailors everywhere. From the beach cat crowds to the America's Cup, multihulls are ubiquitous, and no facet of sailboat chartering is hotter than the cruising catamaran.

The yacht charter industry is, to a large part, responsible for the burgeoning popularity of cruising cats because it challenges boatbuilders and designers to make cruising catamarans comfortable, seaworthy, and easy to sail. Cats in a wide range of sizes are available for bareboat charter in some of the world's greatest cruising areas. Imagine yourself speeding across crystal clear tropical waters upright, stable, and happy to be exactly where you are! No matter where you sail it, a cruising catamaran will provide you, your family, and your friends with great times and lasting memories.

Scudding across the water at exhilarating speeds is just one of the attractions of sailing a catamaran.

Team Adventure was one of six "maxi catamarans" to start The Race on December 31, 2000.

Today's cruising catamarans are fun, safe, and seakindly, with plenty of room on deck and below. They are built with state-of-the art technology, and incorporate modern cruising and liveaboard conveniences in a performance-oriented package.

There are some differences between the operating and handling characteristics of a catamaran and a monohull, so welcome to the ASA114 Cruising Catamaran Standard and this wonderful new book that, by concentrating on those differences, will help you become as proficient with two hulls as you are with one.

In the end, sailing is sailing and, as always, the best thing you can do for your future is practice, practice, practice, and make plans to go cruising and charter a bareboat cruising catamaran in an exotic destination. You are in for a great experience, one that could or should be a real life changing one.

"Sail fast boats fast and have lots of fun!"

Cam Lewis

On her way to third place in The Race, Team Adventure appears to skate across the water rather than sail through it.

Cameron "Cam" Lewis was already a winning dinghy and ocean-racing sailor when, in 1985, he caught the cat bug after finishing a close second in the Worrell 1000, a 1,000-mile dash up the Atlantic coast on off-the-beach catamarans. In 1988, he was on Dennis Conner's winning America's Cup team aboard the catamaran Stars & Stripes, and has sailed on many giant cats, including the 1993 Trophée Jules Verne winner, Explorer, and Team Adventure, which he skippered to third place in The Race in 2001.

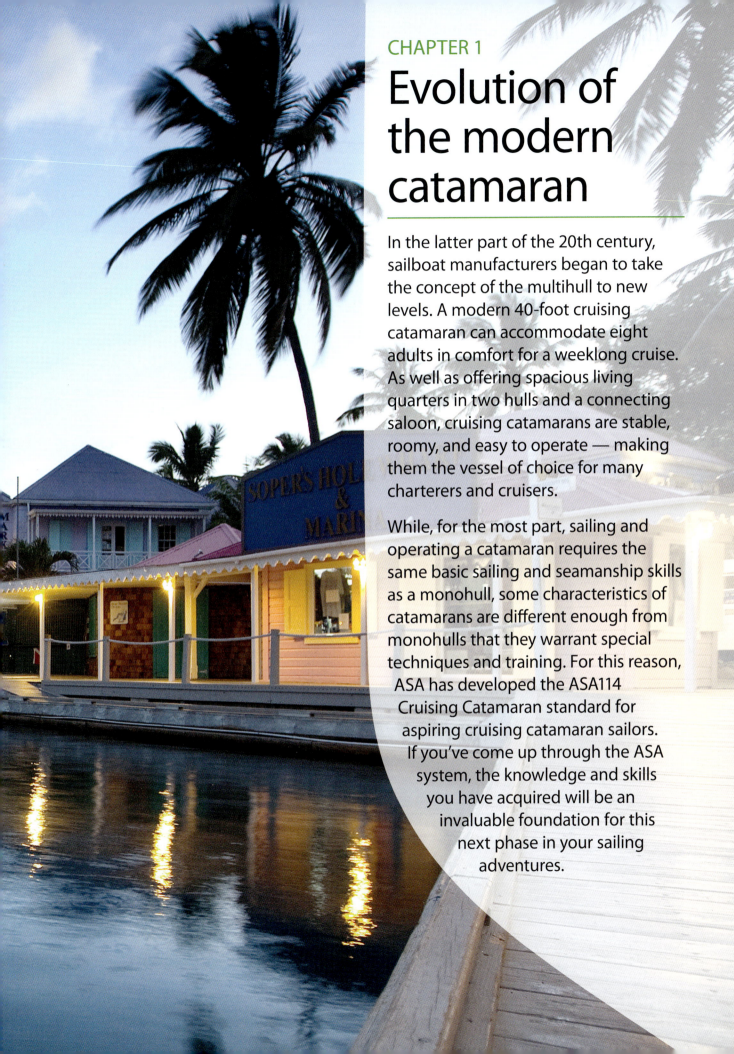

CHAPTER 1

Evolution of the modern catamaran

In the latter part of the 20th century, sailboat manufacturers began to take the concept of the multihull to new levels. A modern 40-foot cruising catamaran can accommodate eight adults in comfort for a weeklong cruise. As well as offering spacious living quarters in two hulls and a connecting saloon, cruising catamarans are stable, roomy, and easy to operate — making them the vessel of choice for many charterers and cruisers.

While, for the most part, sailing and operating a catamaran requires the same basic sailing and seamanship skills as a monohull, some characteristics of catamarans are different enough from monohulls that they warrant special techniques and training. For this reason, ASA has developed the ASA114 Cruising Catamaran standard for aspiring cruising catamaran sailors. If you've come up through the ASA system, the knowledge and skills you have acquired will be an invaluable foundation for this next phase in your sailing adventures.

THE CATAMARAN

A catamaran is a boat that has two hulls connected side-by-side. This type of craft originated with the seafaring cultures of the South Seas — the South Pacific and Indian oceans — and was brought to the attention of Europeans in the 17th century by explorers in search of adventure, discovery, and trade. Technical development of catamarans took place in the Western world, but only slowly, and they remained novelty craft until the 20th century.

INDIA TO THE PACIFIC

In 1697, William Dampier, an English adventurer and buccaneer, wrote from Tamil, India, about the "kattumaram" (literally, "tied wood") he observed there. The vessel was little more than a small raft made of two logs that was able to carry a single man. English explorers of the South Pacific applied this Tamil name to the swift and stable boats, made of two widely separated logs, on which the islanders made voyages between islands and even between archipelagos.

Captain James Cook's logbook from the mid-1700s records a sighting of an enormous two-hulled sailing craft in Tahiti that could carry a hundred warriors. Catamarans and other multihull craft are still used in the Pacific islands and elsewhere by fishermen and for transportation.

Although European visitors to the Pacific islands thought the native craft interesting, they did not find them useful. Catamarans did not have the capacity Europeans required of their ships for carrying heavy cargoes and cannons.

19TH CENTURY AMERICA

Catamarans were reintroduced to the Western world in the 1870s by American yacht designer Nathanael Herreshoff. The innovative naval architect known as "The Wizard of Bristol" began building catamarans to his own designs, and registered the first US patent for a sailing catamaran. The speed and stability of these new vessels soon made them popular pleasure craft in America and Europe, but only for a short while. After Herreshoff's catamaran *Amaryllis*

Nathanael Herreshoff designed and built *Amaryllis* in 1876. She was banned from racing after defeating all the conventional yachts she sailed against. This photo is of the replica built in 1933 that is still on display in the Herreshoff Marine Museum in Bristol, Rhode Island.

James Wharram and Hanneke Boon designed this catamaran to the traditional hull shape in use for centuries in the Pacific islands of Tikopia and Anuta. In the 2008/09 Lapita Voyage, she sailed with a sistership 4,000 miles from the Philippines to Tikopia and Anuta, where the boats were donated to the islanders.

convincingly defeated conventional yachts in the prestigious New York Yacht Club's Centennial Regatta in 1876, the yachting establishment banned catamarans from racing, a ruling that relegated catamarans to the status of novelty boats for decades.

POST WORLD WAR II BOOM

As a banished breed, multihulls were developed outside "traditional" sailing circles, and it wasn't until the mid-20th century that recreational sailors in any numbers began to experiment with them. As disposable incomes began to rise after World War II, interest in recreational boating bloomed. In 1947, the Hawaiian team of Woody Brown and Alfred Kumalae produced *Manu Kai*, the first modern oceangoing catamaran. Their assistant Rudy Choy believed that catamarans were the vessel of the future,

and he became a key figure in the racing and cruising catamaran movement. Choy's *World Cat*, launched in 1965, became the first modern catamaran to circumnavigate the globe.

Englishman James Wharram designed and built his first modern catamaran in 1955, based on his research into ancient Polynesian designs. He crossed the Atlantic to the West Indies in his 24-foot catamaran *Tangaroa*. While there, he built the 40-foot *Rongo* and sailed her back to England via New York. Wharram's designs and kits are still available for purchase, and his cats are seen in harbors around the world.

The 1950s and '60s saw a huge increase in the production of recreational vessels including multihulls, which could be built light and strong, first with modern glues and plywoods and later with fiberglass and other composites. Cruising multihulls

were few in number and diverse in design. Most were unique or home-built to the designs of innovative yet idiosyncratic enthusiasts. Owners and builders sought speed, comfort, and low cost — and too often tried to achieve those goals with cheap construction and lightweight plywood. Ocean races became laboratories for multihull engineering, but the high-profile and often disastrous structural failures that resulted raised considerable doubts about the seaworthiness of catamarans.

After much experimentation in the 1950s, Roland and Francis Prout's Shearwater catamarans easily won races against monohull yachts. In 1954, the Prout brothers converted their Essex, England, boat factory to catamaran production. Prout Catamarans earned the distinction of leading the history of production catamarans for cruising.

DESIGN FREEDOM

Since multihulls were on the fringe of mainstream yachting, their design was not bound by contemporary handicap and racing rules, so multihull designers were able to explore fresh ideas. One example is the large-roach, full-battened mainsail. Widely accepted today on a great variety of boats, it was not allowed under monohull racing rules of the time, but multihull sailors faced no such restriction.

IMAGE BOOST

Multihulls magazine organized a series of World Multihull Symposiums to promote the image and acceptance of multihulls. The first symposium was held in Toronto in 1976, and they continued in Annapolis, Newport, and Miami through 1997. Published transcripts reveal the lively evolution of multihulls in the 20th century, and the promotional goals of the Symposium were achieved.

MODERN PRODUCTION

It was not until the 1980s that naval architects became involved with major manufacturers to create a new generation of practical, attractive, and seaworthy cruising multihulls. Although production cruising catamarans had originated in England with the Prout Brothers, by the 1990s France had taken the lead in the number of boats built. South Africa and Australia also produced quite large numbers, but boatbuilders in the Americas were slower to adopt the trend.

Beginning around the turn of the 21st century, cruising catamarans had developed to where their inherent safety was sufficiently proven for them to become widely accepted. Boosted by growing numbers of cruising catamarans available for charter, and thus "test driving" by potential buyers, the catamaran segment of the boating industry has grown rapidly. New and seasoned sailors alike were, and still are, drawn to them for many reasons.

Catamaran builders today use the latest construction materials, including infusion-molded fiberglass-and-epoxy laminates. Carbon-fiber reinforcements are also used to impart stiffness and strength. Designers have achieved their goal of fitting lots of interior living space in vessels that are light, strong, and capable of high sailing speeds.

THE LEGACY OF HOBIE ALTER

Small catamarans that could be launched off a beach began to appear after World War II as designers exploited wartime advances in molded wood construction.

Several racing classes encouraged development of sails and hulls, among them the C-Class catamaran that competed for a trophy that became popularly known as the Little America's Cup. Fiberglass arrived on the scene in the 1950s and '60s, giving boatbuilders a material that could be used to make multiple identical hulls.

Into this world stepped Hobie Alter, who had already made his name shaping surfboards for his fellow travelers in the Southern California surfing subculture. In 1967, Alter introduced the Hobie 14, a catamaran that could be easily launched and retrieved from a beach by its crew. At beachfront resorts the world over, the Hobie 14, and the even more successful Hobie 16, gave thousands their first taste of sailing.

Hobie Alter, who died in 2014, is fondly remembered by the countless surfers and sailors whose lives he touched through his creations.

THE FUTURE

If the recent past is any indication, the popularity of catamarans will continue to grow. On the cruising front, designers and builders will find ever more ways to merge waterborne with waterfront living. As for racing, the development of foiling technology has already elevated the sport to new levels.

No doubt, too, designers will continue to explore the diversity of forms that two-hulled boats can take. Just as they do with monohulls, some sailors will lean toward the traditional craft and others toward the cutting edge. Choices will be there for all individuals to make.

In 1988, Dennis Conner successfully defended the America's Cup in San Diego with *Stars & Stripes*, a 60-foot catamaran powered by a wing sail.

In the 2013 America's Cup, the AC72 catamarans, powered by wing sails and lifted out of the water on hydrofoils, took performance and speed to new heights.

VOCABULARY

how catamarans and monohulls are constructed and rigged have
w words to the sailor's lexicon. Some of these (and a few familiar terms)
are listed below with their meanings, and many will be more fully explained later.

- **Multihull:** a boat with multiple hulls, either a trimaran or a catamaran
- **Catamaran:** a boat with two widely spaced hulls of equal size
- **Trimaran:** a boat with three hulls, usually a main central hull flanked by amas or floats
- **Bridgedeck:** the deck structure spanning the hulls of a catamaran
- **Nacelle:** a forward projection of the bridgedeck designed to soften the impact of seas beneath the bridgedeck
- **Bridgedeck clearance:** the distance from the water's surface to the underside of the bridgedeck
- **Freeboard:** the height of the hull from the waterline to the deck edge
- **Deckhouse:** the cabin on top of a bridgedeck, typically housing the saloon, nav station, and galley
- **Escape hatch:** a hatch set into the underside of the bridgedeck or the side of a hull in case of capsize

- **Crossbeam:** a beam that connects the hulls of a catamaran
- **Ramp (or catwalk):** a solid walkway along the centerline between the bridgedeck and the forward crossbeam
- **Trampoline:** a taut net spanning the space between the bows of a cruising catamaran
- **Seagull striker:** a braced strut that projects upward on the forward crossbeam to stiffen it against the upward pull of the forestay
- **Dolphin striker:** a braced strut that projects downward from the crossbeam that supports the mast
- **Helm station:** the steering position, usually off centerline and/or elevated to provide visibility
- **Flybridge:** a helm station located on top of the deckhouse
- **Fractional rig:** a rig configuration in which the forestay is attached some distance below the masthead

- **Tripod rig:** a rig configuration made up of a forestay and shrouds that are far enough aft that a backstay is not needed
- **Diamond stays:** wire rigging braced by spreaders, or struts, in a diamond shape that keeps the mast in column
- **Roach:** area at the leech of a sail that extends outside a straight line between the head and clew
- **Bridle:** a pair of lines used to spread the load from a central connecting point to two separate points (used when anchored or moored or when towing or being towed)
- **Fixed keel:** a fin-shaped appendage on the bottom of a hull that provides directional stability and lateral resistance when sailing
- **Daggerboard:** a board that can be lowered through a trunk in the hull to provide lateral resistance when sailing
- **Twin-screw vessel:** a vessel with two engines and two propellers (screws)

The bridgedeck clearance on this catamaran is not very high, but the nacelle that protrudes downward from the bridgedeck softens the impact of waves.

A flybridge places the helm station and all the sail controls on a higher level, leaving more space in the cockpit for lounging and entertaining.

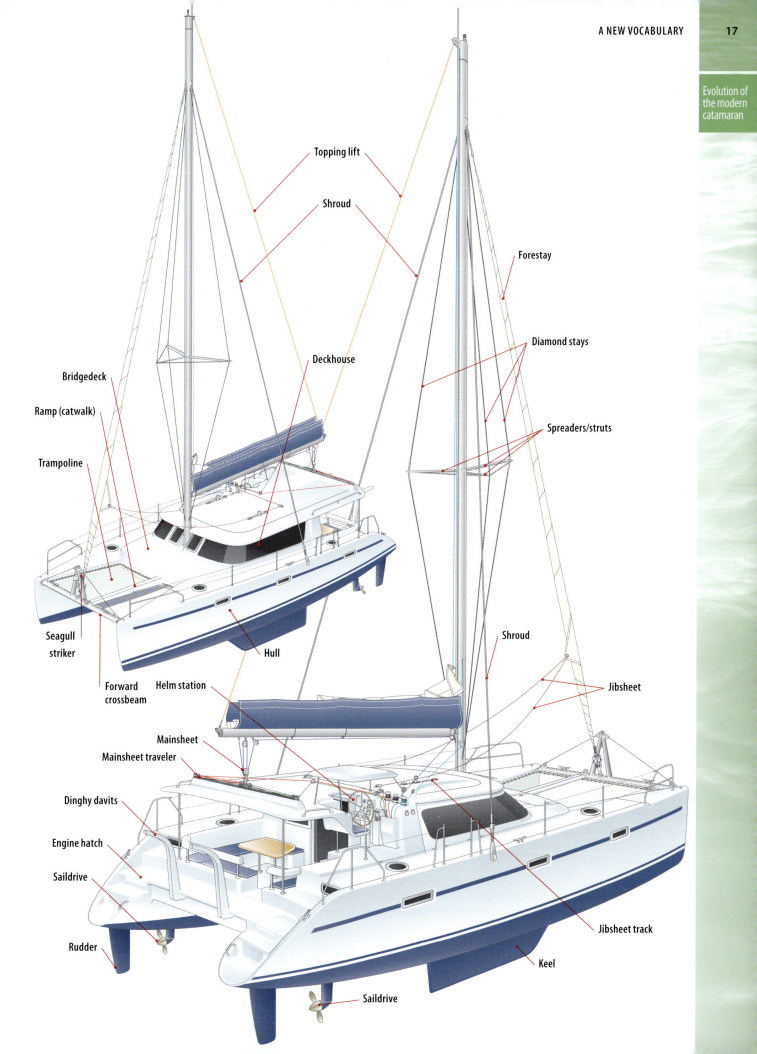

Topping lift

Shroud

Forestay

Diamond stays

Deckhouse

Bridgedeck

Ramp (catwalk)

Spreaders/struts

Trampoline

Shroud

Jibsheet

Seagull
striker

Hull

Forward
crossbeam

Helm station

Mainsheet

Mainsheet traveler

Dinghy davits

Engine hatch

Saildrive

Jibsheet track

Rudder

Keel

Saildrive

GOING FROM ONE HULL TO TWO

A debate about the relative merits of catamarans and monohulls can sometimes become lively, as sailors are notorious for holding strong views. Just as sports cars, utility vehicles, and sedans all have their fans, boats of different types appeal to different sailors. Like their automotive counterparts, boats of different styles and designs have their trade-offs.

CATAMARAN SAILING SPEED

Legendary yacht designer L. Francis Herreshoff said, "The fun of sailing is proportional to the speed of sailing." Based on that sentiment, catamaran sailing delivers fun in abundance.

Catamarans designed strictly for performance, whether the off-the-beach variety or the larger ocean racers, will take the wind out of the sails of any similarly purposed monohull. Although with their comfort-oriented amenities, cruising catamarans don't have the same all around speed edge, they far outpace cruising monohulls of similar length

when reaching. This is due mainly to three inherent differences: stability, weight, and hull shape.

■ **Stability:** A sailboat's speed depends on how much sail power it can stand up to, and that is directly related to its stability. A monohull depends on wide beam for initial stability and a heavy ballasted keel for ultimate stability. Both features create drag. A catamaran derives its stability from the buoyancy and wide separation of its two hulls.

■ **Hull shape:** Sailors have long known that a slender hull is "easily driven" but is less inherently stable than a wide one.

The large number of catamarans in favorite harbors testifies to their popularity, especially among charterers.

Several crewmembers can live aboard a catamaran without rubbing elbows, and loose items tend to stay where they are placed because the boat stays fairly level, even under way.

Because catamarans don't rely on the individual hulls for stability, they can be given hulls that are narrow for their length compared to monohulls.

■ **Weight:** Heavy is slow. Since they don't need ballast for stability (see "Sailboat Stability," page 24), catamarans can be light and fast.

GOOD BEHAVIOR

Another aspect that is attractive to some sailors is the behavior of catamarans under sail and at rest. Because of their high stability, catamarans heel very little when sailing and they are not prone to rolling when at anchor or on a mooring. These characteristics make living aboard somewhat less challenging than it sometimes is on a monohull.

SENSITIVITY TO LOADING

Overloading any boat will cause the hull or hulls to sink deeper in the water. The resultant additional frictional drag impairs sailing performance. Without the concentrated weight of a ballasted keel, a catamaran is more sensitive than a monohull keelboat to longitudinal (forward and aft) loading.

Excess weight in the bow or stern affects the way the boat pitches (rocks fore and aft) in a seaway, and can aggravate the tendency of some designs to hobbyhorse when sailing upwind in waves. Overloading in the bows could have the additional undesirable effect of causing the bows to bury in big seas.

PERFORMANCE VS. COMFORT

The combination of slender hulls, light weight, and high stability makes catamarans potentially fast. However, features and amenities that make catamarans comfortable cruisers tend to add weight, which works against their achieving the same speeds as high-performance catamarans. Within the cruising catamaran genre, yacht designers continually strive to strike the optimal balance between performance, speed, volume, and comfort.

Due its high inherent stability, a cruising catamaran, even one loaded with creature comforts, can show a good turn of speed when sailing on a close reach at a very small angle of heel.

The price of higher performance is narrower hulls (less space for cabins), and lighter weight (fewer onboard amenities).

SIZE COMPARISONS

When weighing the characteristics of a cruising catamaran against those of a cruising monohull, size is important. If it's a matter of choosing between two boats, it's not realistic to compare a catamaran to a monohull of the same length. A 40-foot cruising catamaran will have accommodations to match those of at least a 45-foot monohull and, fully equipped, it will weigh as much also. Due to the catamaran's stability (see page 24), the loads on the standing rigging, sails, and running rigging (and therefore winches) will at times be greater than on a monohull of similar length.

Compared to a monohull of similar size, a catamaran has much more deck space for crew activities.

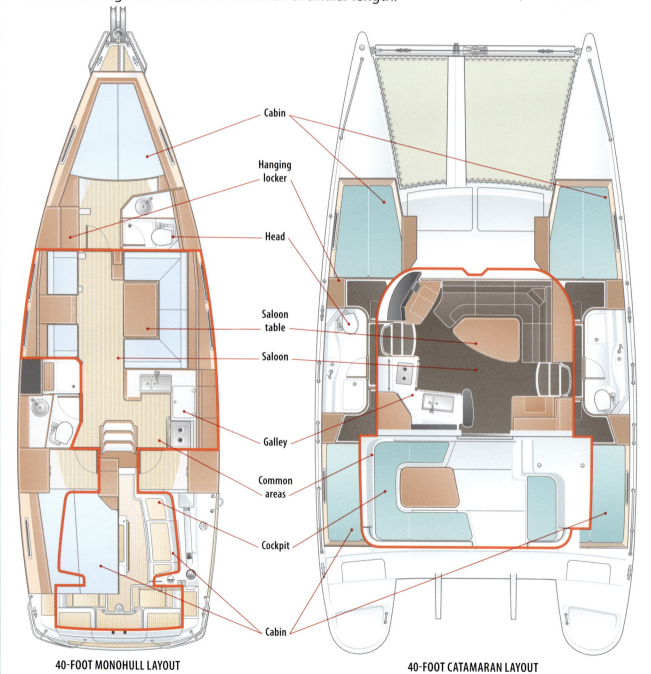

Cabin

Hanging locker

Head

Saloon table

Saloon

Galley

Common areas

Cockpit

Cabin

40-FOOT MONOHULL LAYOUT

40-FOOT CATAMARAN LAYOUT

A CRUISING PLATFORM

Catamarans have many features that are enormously attractive to sailors from the standpoint of cruising comfort.

■ **Space:** In the roomy surroundings, on deck and below, everyone on board can be comfortable throughout a cruise. The foredeck, cockpit, saloon, and cabins provide a variety of places for crew to gather in groups large and small.

■ **Privacy:** Sleeping cabins and en-suite head facilities in the two hulls, separated as they are by the common areas in the deckhouse (and by air and water beneath it), have a high level of privacy.

■ **Light and ventilation:** The raised saloon with its abundant windows and sliding "patio doors" affords light and ventilation throughout the deckhouse. Hatches overhead and portlights in the hull sides cross-ventilate the cabins.

■ **All-around views:** Large windows provide a panoramic view from the

A cruising catamaran has abundant space for lounging and dining, and even the outside areas are mostly sheltered from the sun and showers. When the weather closes in, the crew stays dry while enjoying the view from the deckhouse.

deckhouse and everyone benefits. The navigator can check on the boat's surroundings (some designs even provide an inside helm station) and the cook has a spacious, well lit, and stable galley for preparing meals. The outside helm station also offers some protection, and the cockpit canopy shelters everyone from rain and excessive sunlight.

■ **Heeling:** A catamaran heels very little under sail, and this steady level environment reduces crew fatigue on longer passages and takes some of the strain out of boat-handling tasks in stronger winds.

■ **Safety:** Yacht manufacturing standards in some countries require that multihulls be unsinkable. This is achieved with watertight bulkheads and high-density structural foam. The absence of ballast helps. Even in a boat not built to this requirement, a hole in a hull should not sink a catamaran, as the second hull will provide enough buoyancy to keep it afloat. Fast passage speeds and the less tiring low-heel operating environment also contribute to safety.

In the same wind and on the same point of sail, a catamaran remains nearly upright while a monohull heels.

THE TWO-HULL DIFFERENCE

As with anything in life, choosing a boat to sail, or perhaps eventually to own, raises questions about priorities and preferences. Catamarans and monohulls offer many of the same enticements — the thrill of sailing, the challenge of navigating new waters, and the independent life on the water — but with emphasis on different aspects of the cruising life.

SAILING

While any boat's sailing abilities are affected by the same factors — weight, stability, power (from the sails), and hull form — the balance of those factors is different between monohulls and catamarans. Sailing fast, as well as being fun, gets you to your destination more quickly, whether you're seeking a lively waterfront restaurant or a safe harbor.

■ **Overall performance:** All sailboats perform well when operating within their load-carrying capacities. However, since a big factor in catamarans' sailing performance is their lightness, weight added in the form of appliances and amenities to enhance cruising comfort is a mixed blessing. It not only causes a loss in performance, it also reduces the bridgedeck clearance (see page 16), which can affect comfort in waves.

■ **Sailing to windward:** Draft is a key factor in upwind sailing performance. Monohulls achieve the ability to point high with deep keels designed to generate hydrodynamic lift. Catamarans designed for high performance use daggerboards to generate lift, and may outsail monohulls to windward. Cruising catamarans are usually fitted with less efficient shoal-draft keels, so their windward performance is inhibited.

■ **Reaching:** Cruising catamarans perform at their best when reaching, and it is when sailing at reaching angles that they consistently show their sterns to cruising monohulls.

■ **Running:** Cruising catamarans are no speed demons when running, especially in light air, in part because the tripod rig (see page 16) does not permit the mainsail to be fully eased. Mainsails on many monohulls are similarly restricted, but usually less so, by swept-back spreaders on the mast. Sailors of both types of boat can often make better time by broad reaching (see page 50).

■ **Daggerboards and centerboards:** When monohulls and catamarans employ centerboards or daggerboards, it's usually for different reasons. Catamarans use daggerboards instead of deep keels to generate hydrodynamic lift when sailing to windward. Monohulls primarily use centerboards (or lifting keels) so they

Even when the wind is up, a catamaran "stands on its feet." Its crew doesn't have to sit braced in the cockpit and can move about on deck (albeit cautiously) with relative ease.

While catamarans offer a lot of living space, they also take up a lot of room. Finding dock space can be a challenge as many marina slips are not wide enough for them.

can access shallow water while retaining good upwind sailing performance.

- **Feedback when overpowered:** On a monohull, excessive heeling is a sure sign the boat is overpowered and it's time to reduce sail. Because a catamaran heels very little, the helmsman and crew have little direct feedback to indicate when it's overpowered. That means they must pay close attention to the wind speed if they are to reef in a timely manner.

- **Motion:** As well as heeling far less than monohulls, catamarans have a completely different motion in seas. Each wave hits twice — once on each hull — resulting in an awkward, quick, jerking motion. This upsets some sailors' stomachs, but queasy crew do find it easier to move around on the generally level platform of a catamaran than on the tilted world of a monohull.

- **Draft:** Since cruising catamarans, including those fitted with keels, don't draw much water, they can explore and anchor in shallow creeks and bays that deep-draft monohulls have to avoid.

PRACTICALITIES

When it comes to owning, or even chartering, a catamaran, the differences from monohulls have practical impacts on aspects from sailing to budgeting.

- **Cost:** Cruising catamarans cost more

to build than monohulls of comparable size. This is due to the amount of material and labor used in the construction of their twin hulls, the additional structure of the bridgedeck and saloon, the outfit and furniture, the more rugged mast and rigging, and onboard systems that in some cases are duplicated.

- **Maintenance:** Along with the initial cost, maintenance expenses can add up for a catamaran, given the multiple systems and the scarcity of boatyards with haulout equipment that can handle the wide beam.

- **Systems redundancy:** Duplication of some systems in each hull allows redundancy should any single system break down. This is especially valuable in the event of an engine failure.

- **Size:** A catamaran's wide beam permits the extra living space but is a disadvantage when berthing, as many marinas do not have the extra dockage space catamarans need. When larger berths are available, they are likely to be priced accordingly.

- **Boat handling:** Maneuvering a catamaran under power in protected waters and light winds when docking or anchoring is greatly simplified by having two engines and two propellers. A monohull can only be maneuvered with anything like the same precision if it's fitted with a bow thruster.

- **Deck work:** Broad decks that stay mostly level facilitate sail handling and other deck work.

- **High freeboard:** Cruising catamarans have high freeboard to ensure standing headroom in the hulls. The windage of the hulls, combined with that of a large deckhouse, is considerably more than that of a monohull. It inhibits sailing performance to windward and adds difficulty to maneuvering under power in close quarters and strong winds. Windage should also be factored in when figuring the size of anchor to use and the scope when setting it. High freeboard can make getting on and off the boat difficult, especially at low floating docks.

- **Inability to self-right:** In the extremely unlikely event that a cruising catamaran capsizes, the stability offered by the hulls makes it all but impossible to right. (On the bright side, it won't sink.) Most monohulls will self-right and survive a rollover, but will sink if they suffer a major breach of the hull.

- **Aesthetics:** Few catamaran designs achieve the long low profile regarded as the "classic" yacht look, but they have evolved their own aesthetic. They might be compared with monohulls in the way SUVs are compared with sedans and sports cars, giving up sleekness for a more bulky but robust appearance that speaks to their superior power.

The catamaran's appearance brings to mind aerodynamic designs of the age of space travel, while the schooner in the background owes its aesthetics to the age of sail. Both styles have ardent followers.

SAILBOAT STABILITY: ONE HULL VS. TWO

The term stability is used when discussing a sailboat's ability to withstand the wind's force and not capsize. Catamaran capsizes in high-profile races created an impression that all catamarans are unstable. They are **not**. The discussion that follows is beyond the scope of the ASA114 standard, but is provided because catamaran sailors need to understand that their boats achieve their stability in a different way from monohulls.

WEIGHT AND FORM FACTORS

A boat derives its stability from its form (shape), its weight, and the distribution of that weight. The most obvious difference between a catamaran and a monohull is their shapes — the catamaran has two hulls, widely separated, to the monohull's one. This gives the catamaran high initial stability (at small angles of heel) based on its form. But form stability has limits.

BASIC STABILITY

Anyone who steps into a long narrow boat like a canoe or kayak learns quickly that it is "tippy," or unstable — you have to be careful to keep your weight in the middle so as not to capsize it. A rowboat or skiff is usually wider and therefore less *tender*. The bigger and heavier the boat, the less tender, or the more stable, it is.

When you add a sail to a boat, as on a sailing dinghy, you have to balance the tipping effect of the wind on the sail — heeling — with your weight, by sitting on the windward side. Adding ballast to the boat, either in the bottom of the hull or hung below the hull in a keel, makes the boat more stable yet.

Seafarers of Oceania discovered that, by lashing together two unstable dugout canoes (made by hollowing out tree trunks), they could make a very stable craft. And the farther apart the two hulls, the "stiffer," or more stable, it was.

CENTERS OF BUOYANCY AND GRAVITY

Any floating body, when no external force is acting on it, assumes a position of equilibrium where the center of gravity (CG) and the center of the immersed volume, called the center of buoyancy (CB), are aligned vertically — one directly above the other. When subjected to a force that disturbs that equilibrium, the

floating body seeks a new equilibrium. A sailboat, when subjected to the force of the wind on the sails, heels. As it does so, its CB moves to leeward until the boat's total weight, acting through its CG, balances that force.

The horizontal distance between the CG and the CB is called the righting arm, and the product of the boat's weight multiplied by the righting arm is the righting moment. (To picture righting arm and righting moment, think of children on a seesaw. To balance a small child sitting on one end, a heavier child must sit nearer the pivot point. They exert the same righting moment but at righting arms of different lengths.)

RIGHTING ARM

When a boat is upright, the righting arm is zero. As the boat heels, the righting arm becomes longer until it reaches a

maximum, then diminishes as it heels farther. When the righting arm reaches zero again, the boat is at its limit of positive stability (LPS). If it heels any farther, it will capsize.

The longer the righting arm, then, the higher the righting moment. A longer righting arm can be achieved by adding weight low down and lowering the CG or by modifying the boat's form so the CB moves farther to leeward when the boat heels. On a monohull keelboat, ballast in the keel is used to locate the CG where it achieves the desired righting arms as the boat heels. (On a sailing dinghy, you adjust the righting arm — and the righting moment — by how far outboard you sit or hike.)

On a modern offshore cruising monohull, the righting arm is at its maximum at 50 to 60 degrees of heel, and the limit of positive stability is 120 degrees or higher.

CATAMARAN STABILITY

When a catamaran is floating level, its CG is directly above its CB, halfway between the hulls. As it heels, the leeward hull immerses, the windward hull emerges, and the CB moves toward the leeward hull — the righting arm gets longer. A catamaran's initial stability is very high

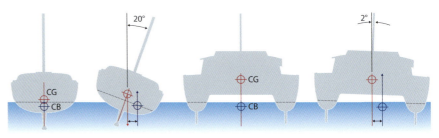

At rest, a boat floats in a stable position with its center of gravity (CG) and center of buoyancy (CB) in the same vertical line. As a sailboat heels, its CB moves to leeward, creating a righting arm between the CB and the CG. Note that, due to the very different way buoyancy is distributed in the monohull and the catamaran, while the righting arms for both boats in this diagram are equal, their heel angles are very different: 20 degrees for the monohull, 2 degrees for the catamaran.

because a small angle of heel causes the righting arm to lengthen significantly. However, compared to a monohull, the maximum righting arm comes at a very small angle of heel — less than 10 degrees — at which the windward hull "flies" and the leeward hull provides all the buoyancy. The limit of positive stability is in the region of 70 degrees.

Weight is a major factor in stability. The heavier the boat (monohull or multihull), the greater the righting moment for any given length of righting arm.

THE CAPSIZE

The monohull's ability to heel is a safety valve. As it heels, it presents less sail area to the wind, reducing the heeling force. A cruising monohull will not capsize under wind force alone because the sails are in the water long before it reaches its LPS. It takes a big breaking wave to capsize a monohull keelboat.

A cruising catamaran does not have this safety valve, and heel angle alone

A skilled racing crew might fly a hull to gain extra speed, but do not attempt this in your cruising home.

does not give sufficient warning that it's overpowered. Catamaran sailors must be alert to the strength of the wind at all times because, if the windward hull flies, the boat is at risk of capsizing. (Racing catamarans often fly a hull while sailing,

but that's a calculated risk experienced racing sailors are willing to take.)

Well below the capsize threshold, gusts of wind can generate sudden high forces on the rig that a catamaran cannot relieve by heeling. Sails, sheets, and gear must be able to withstand these shock loads.

Modern cruising catamarans are highly resistant to capsize. It would take severe wind and sea conditions to invert one — the same sea state in which a monohull might also be vulnerable. Most cruising sailors plan their voyages with care so as to avoid such conditions.

STATIC VS. DYNAMIC STABILITY

The discussion above is limited to the static state, i.e, without regard to the dynamics of waves or the boat's motion. A sailboat is rarely in a static state and waves, especially large waves, do affect its stability. However, the static numbers are a good indication of a sailboat's stability in most conditions a prudent cruising sailor is likely to encounter.

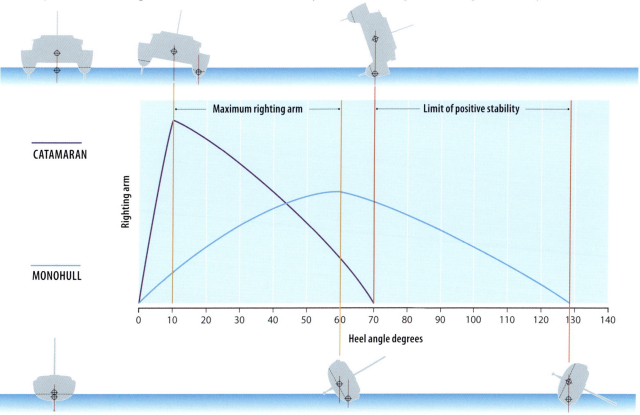

A boat's righting moment, a measure of its resistance to heeling at any angle of heel, is its weight multiplied by the righting arm. A catamaran's maximum righting moment is much greater than that of a monohull of the same weight, but diminishes quickly at greater heel angles, and its limit of positive stability occurs at a much smaller angle than a monohull's.

CHAPTER 2

Catamaran essentials

When you first started sailing, you spent some time looking around the boat, learning about the deck hardware, rigging, sails, and the domestic and safety systems. You will do the same thing the first time you board a catamaran. Most of the fixtures, above deck and below, will be familiar, but some will be new and some will be in unfamiliar places.

Before casting off the docklines for the first time, explore your new cruising catamaran from bow to stern, on deck and below, to make sure you know where all the essential operating systems are and how they work, from the anchoring setup, to the sheet winches, and to the switches for the electric water pump and the lights. If you're chartering, ask your charter briefer lots of questions and take notes. At the first opportunity, go through the boat again, with your notes, and point out important features to your crew.

This chapter gives an overview of the structural and domestic features of a cruising catamaran.

ACCOMMODATIONS AND AMENITIES

Two hulls and a connecting deckhouse allow for a lot of volume to devote to living quarters, and designers of cruising catamarans have devised countless imaginative ways to use it all efficiently. All that space means there's plenty of room for creature comforts too.

INTERIOR OPTIONS

Catamaran builders offer a variety of interior layouts to suit the differing needs of owners and charterers. Space in the hulls is mostly dedicated to staterooms and heads. A private owner might choose an arrangement where one hull is dedicated to an owner's stateroom, a spacious head and shower, and perhaps a settee or some office space. A version of the same model intended for charter would usually have more sleeping cabins and heads and fewer storage areas. Many charter catamarans have a head for each sleeping cabin, which greatly enhances privacy. Lockers or drawers are often fitted under the berths. The forepeaks in the hulls are used for storage (of light items only) and sometimes an extra berth.

The primary interior living space is in the deckhouse, which usually contains the dining area, the navigation station, the electrical control panel, and stairways that lead to the sleeping cabins. In the more common "galley-up" style, it also houses the galley. In a "galley-down" design, the galley is in a hull.

OUTSIDE AREAS

In fine weather, much of the social activity takes place outdoors in the cockpit and surrounding area. Sheltered from the sun under a rigid roof or soft Bimini but open to the breeze, the cockpit has abundant seating for the entire crew and is perfect for relaxing and dining. The aft decks of the hulls step down to the waterline and provide easy

A spacious sheltered cockpit area ensures gracious outdoor living with fresh air and panoramic views.

access for swimming and for boarding dinghies and water toys such as paddleboards. The swim platforms are also a great place for taking an after-swim freshwater shower.

The airy interior of a catamaran's deckhouse has the atmosphere of a beach cottage — a far cry from the dark wood-paneled, dimly lit saloon in a traditional yacht.

The vast deck provides lots of places for crew to engage in a variety of activities at the same time — rinsing off after a swim, catching a little sun, or phoning home.

Some catamaran designs have sliding doors leading from the saloon to another lounge area forward of the deckhouse. Even without this feature, the bridgedeck area forward of the saloon is the place to sit to watch the scenery unfold. Children of all ages enjoy the trampoline for lounging or fish watching when the boat is at anchor, but it must be treated with caution when the boat is under way as it flexes unpredictably.

HELM STATION

The helm station on a catamaran is often situated just aft of the deckhouse or above it on a flybridge. An elevated station gives a good all-around view but separates the helmsman from the crew in the cockpit.

Very often, the sails are controlled entirely from the helm station. This arrangement works well for a skippered charter but a station that's more in the cockpit allows better interaction among the crew, although the view from the helm can be more constrained.

Some higher-performance catamarans have twin helm stations well aft, one on each hull. While this position is good for a helmsman who likes to feel how the boat is sailing, it is exposed to the elements. It might also limit the helmsman's view while docking, depending on which side the engine controls are located relative to the dock.

On a catamaran, the helm station might be aft on the hull (in which case there is usually one on each hull), against the bulkhead and elevated above the cockpit, or even inside the deckhouse. Each position has its points depending on the purpose for which the boat was designed and the preferences of its sailors.

STRUCTURE

Catamarans present special engineering challenges in hull structure, hull connections, and rig. How these problems are solved in individual designs influences the appearance, sailing performance and, in cruising catamarans, use of space both on deck and inside the boat.

FORCE MATTERS

The wind, sea, and sail forces on a catamaran act in very different ways than on a monohull, in large part due to the wide spacing of its twin hulls. In big seas, for example, the hulls might be supported at different points on the same wave, which creates torque between the hulls. Catamarans must, therefore, be built with specific components and reinforced in critical areas to maintain structural integrity.

A full bridgedeck that extends most of the way to the bows provides space for cruising accommodations.

HULL DESIGN

Catamarans are able to achieve high sailing speeds through a combination of easily-driven slender hulls, light weight, and enough stability to permit carrying lots of sail. Slender hulls, though, are more sensitive to added weight than wider hulls and this must be borne in mind when loading a catamaran for cruising.

Every pound added to a narrow hull sinks it deeper than it would a wider hull of the same displacement. Wetted surface increases in proportion with immersion, and with added wetted surface comes increased drag on the hull. Also, the deeper immersion of the hulls reduces the bridgedeck clearance, which affects the boat's performance in waves and the comfort of those on board.

Beamier (wider) hulls are more tolerant of added weight and can house roomier cabins than narrow hulls. Designers of cruising catamarans lean toward beamier hulls for their greater volume for living space, even if that comes at the cost of some loss in performance.

CROSSBEAMS

The two hulls of a catamaran are joined together by crossbeams. To withstand the torque created between two hulls immersed in different waves, these crossbeams and their connections to the hulls must be very strong.

A common arrangement is a forward crossbeam, an aft crossbeam, and a crossbeam to support the mast. In cruising catamarans, the aft crossbeam and the support for the mast are usually incorporated into the structure of the

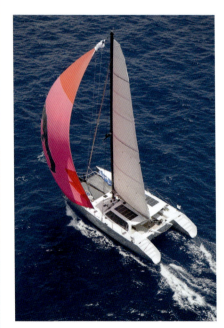

When seeking higher performance, designers save weight with a shorter solid bridgedeck and more extensive trampolines between the bows.

This catamaran, which has an open bridgedeck, is light, fast, beachable, and well-suited to coastal cruising in shallow waters. The cabins and galley are in the hulls and the bridgedeck is open to the breeze, although a roof and clear plastic drop curtains keep out rain. The aft crossbeam ties the hulls and bridgedeck together and supports the mainsheet traveler.

The forward crossbeam (red circle), which connects the two hulls at the bow, is braced by the seagull striker (inset).
A trampoline fills the space between the hulls and the anchor chain runs along a ramp (catwalk) that is also a walkway.

bridgedeck, which is integrated with the hulls as a single unit.

On many designs, the mainsheet traveler is mounted on the aft crossbeam to take advantage of the extra structural rigidity in that area.

BRIDGEDECK

A catamaran's bridgedeck is the deck that spans the area between the hulls. Since a deck adds weight, the extent of the bridgedeck is suggestive of a catamaran's expected performance under sail. Not everyone agrees on the descriptive terms used for different bridgedeck types.

Beach catamarans, like Hobie Cats, and full-on racing cats are often described as having an *open bridgedeck*. It might be partially rigid or even non-structural with the crossbeams providing the structure.

The term *full bridgedeck,* when used in reference to a cruising catamaran, might mean it extends all the way to the bows or simply that it supports a roomy cockpit and a spacious *deckhouse* that extends over the hulls. When the bridgedeck does not extend all the way to the bows, a lightweight *trampoline* is normally fitted to fill the space between them.

A catamaran designed more for high performance than comfort might have a small shelter on a short bridgedeck, sometimes called a *partial bridgedeck,*

while the berths, galley, and head are all in the hulls. This configuration is seen on some ocean-racing catamarans.

NACELLE

On aircraft, a nacelle is a pod or a casing enclosing an engine. On a catamaran, the term refers to a blister-shaped protrusion on the underside of the bridgedeck that, on some models, extends some distance toward the forward crossbeam. A nacelle can soften the impact of waves, and the extra volume inside it is used for storage, water and fuel tanks, or to extend the living space.

SEAGULL STRIKER

On a monohull, the forestay is attached at or near the stem, where the hull sides and the deck form a very strong and rigid structure. On a catamaran, the forestay is attached at the middle of the forward crossbeam, which would bend upward under the forestay tension if it weren't suitably reinforced. The *seagull striker* provides that reinforcement, often in the form of an A-shaped metal fabrication braced by steel cables.

RAMPS AND TRAMPOLINES

The forestay also pulls aft on the crossbeam, and on some models a *ramp* or *catwalk* joining the center of the

crossbeam to the bridgedeck provides reinforcement in this direction. The ramp provides a stable walkway along the boat's centerline between the forward crossbeam and the bridgedeck.

Most cruising catamarans have a trampoline forward between the hulls. Usually made of heavy netting or woven webbing, it's attached to the hulls, the forward crossbeam, and the forward edge of the bridgedeck. Larger waves wash through it, reducing the slamming effect and the potential for tripping. A trampoline is lighter than a rigid deck, so it helps reduce the weight forward.

A trampoline allows crew to work with sails (although it's hard to maintain balance on a "tramp" under way) and is a great place for basking and play when at anchor. It's not a good place to hang out when the boat is moving through waves.

Since constant exposure to sunlight and seawater can degrade the tramp, it should be inspected on a regular basis.

DOLPHIN STRIKER

The center crossbeam supports the downward pressure from the mast, and requires substantial reinforcement. On beach and racing cats, this is achieved with a *dolphin striker*, which is structurally similar to a seagull striker but projects downward beneath the main crossbeam.

On cruising catamarans, the structure within the bridgedeck, with additional reinforcement from a bulkhead, performs the function of the dolphin striker.

The dolphin striker on this beach cat stiffens the crossbeam that supports the mast.

SPARS, RIGGING, AND SAILS

With very few exceptions, catamarans are rigged with a single mast, a mainsail, and a single headsail that's usually on a roller furler. Many boats are also equipped to fly an asymmetrical spinnaker, sometimes from a small sprit that projects from the forward crossbeam. The wide stance, high stability, and structural demands of a catamaran require — and allow — the mast to be supported somewhat differently than it is on a monohull.

STANDING RIGGING

On a monohull, the mast is supported by the boat's structural backbone or keel, either directly, if the mast is stepped on the keel, or via a compression post if the mast is stepped on deck. A catamaran does not have the same backbone structure and the mast, which in many cases is stepped on the bridgedeck, is supported by a crossbeam integrated into the bridgedeck structure.

A catamaran's broad beam makes a wide enough base that the shrouds meet the mast at a suitable angle without the use of spreaders. And if the shrouds are attached well aft of the mast, a backstay is not needed. The resulting three-legged system of forestay and upper shrouds is often referred to as a *tripod rig*.

Large righting moments that result from a catamaran's stability translate into high tension in the forestay and shrouds and high compression loads on the mast. Systems of *diamond stays* supported by spreaders and struts (seen in a variety of arrangements) act as trusses to keep the mast straight and in column.

SAIL PLAN

A cruising catamaran's sail plan is typically a fractional rig with a large full-battened mainsail and a roller-furling jib. "Fractional" refers to the height, 7/8 or 3/4, for example, at which the forestay is attached to the mast expressed as a fraction of the mast height.

The fractional rig has become common on modern cruising boats of all types because of its aerodynamic efficiency and because it is easier to manage under sail than a masthead sail plan. With the backstay-less tripod rig, catamaran designers can easily add the desired sail area in a full-battened mainsail with a large roach.

The shorter forestay also has less inherent sag than a stay attached at the masthead, and this helps to reduce induced draft. The smaller jib makes tacking quicker and easier and it generates less force, thereby reducing the load on the forward crossbeam.

THE BOOM

The boom is sized to carry the sailing loads generated by the large mainsail. Since few catamarans have a rigid boom vang, a strong topping lift is needed to support the combined weight of the boom and the furled mainsail.

FREEBOARD EFFECT ON SAILS

Due to the freeboard and the high deckhouse, the sails, especially the mainsail, are relatively high above the water compared to a monohull. This results in an elevated center of effort, which affects stability to a small degree.

While the tripod arrangement of a forestay and one shroud each side holds the mast up, a system of spreaders, struts, and diamond stays stiffens the mast to hold it in column.

In the absence of a backstay, mainsail area can be added in the roach — the part of the sail outside the straight line from head to clew — instead of by making the mast taller.

KEELS AND DAGGERBOARDS

Catamarans need some means to limit leeway. The majority of today's cruising catamarans do this with long keels that do not need to be very deep because they remain close to vertical at all times, unlike a monohull's keel that loses effective draft when it heels. The keels also offer some protection to the hulls, rudders, and running gear if the boat should run aground.

To achieve better windward ability, instead of keels, some catamarans are fitted with daggerboards that generate lift and lateral resistance. They are not without their drawbacks: Daggerboards are usually manually operated, they can break and potentially cause structural damage around the trunk if the boat is grounded with the boards down, and the trunks take up cabin space. Many enthusiastic catamaran sailors believe the gain in performance is worth the added complication, cost, and other compromises that dagger-boards entail.

Daggerboard

STEERING

A cruising catamaran has two rudders, one mounted under each hull. They are connected, very often by a tie rod inside the boat, so they operate together. The principal drive mechanism from the steering wheel to the rudder is usually a chain connected to cables that are in turn connected to a quadrant on one rudder stock or tillers on both. A removable deck plate over the top of a rudder stock (sometimes both) allows the emergency tiller to be attached.

The rudders are smaller than those on monohulls but, because the boat heels very little and there are two of them, they are quite efficient except at very low speeds. During maneuvers at low speed under power, most of the steering is done with the propellers.

While most cruising catamarans have a single helm station, some models have one on each stern. On these boats, some components of the steering system are duplicated.

Electronic autopilots work very well on catamarans. The long narrow hulls track well and the lack of heeling tends to keep weather helm down, reducing the work an autopilot has to do.

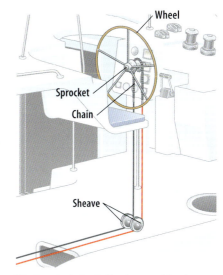

Wheel steering is often bulkhead-mounted, but the same principles and components are used as on a monohull.

The emergency tiller fits on either one of the rudder stocks, whichever is appropriate in the circumstances.

When sailing on a broad reach or running, daggerboards are usually raised to reduce drag. When sailing to windward or close reaching, daggerboards are lowered to create lift and reduce leeway (see inset).

In many steering systems, a tie rod connects the two rudders. A separate tiller is fitted for the autopilot drive.

SYSTEMS

Catamaran systems — mechanical, plumbing, and electrical — are for the most part the same as those on monohulls. However, since they must serve two hulls and a large saloon with many amenities, all are more complex and some may be duplicated.

PROPULSION

A major duplication is in the propulsion systems. Most cruising cats have an engine and the associated accessories and running gear in each hull. While two engines bring many advantages when handling the boat under power, they also require twice the maintenance.

ENGINES AND RUNNING GEAR

Engines on catamarans are the same marine diesels that are found on monohulls and have the same fuel, electrical, cooling, and exhaust systems. On larger cats, the engines are usually housed aft of the accommodations in dedicated compartments with deck hatches for access. On some boats, they are beneath the berths in the aft cabins.

Many cats are fitted with saildrive systems rather than propellers on conventional propeller shafts that exit the hull through a stern tube. The diesel engines are the same but the saildrive unit protrudes vertically downward from the hull and looks like the bottom half of an outboard motor.

TWO-ENGINE ADVANTAGE

The most important benefit conferred by two engines is the maneuvering agility made possible by independently driven propellers. This "twin screw" effect is amplified on a catamaran by the wide horizontal separation of the propellers.

Another advantage of twin engines is having redundancy in case one of them fails to operate. It's also possible to use just one engine to save fuel and wear and tear on the engines. Motorsailing using just one engine will still give the extra boost of speed that generates valuable apparent wind.

....

TIP *Because you have a choice of running either one or both engines, keep a log of each engine's hours to balance their use and help you to estimate fuel consumption.*

....

THE FUEL SYSTEM

The fuel tanks might be in the hulls or in the bridgedeck area. There might be one tank shared by both engines, two tanks shared by both engines, or one tank for each engine. Each engine has its own primary and secondary fuel filters. **NOTE** A diesel engine draws more fuel from the tank than it uses, and returns the excess fuel to the tank. If the return fuel goes to a tank that is full, it will overflow via the vent and go into the sea, which is a problem on many levels and can result in substantial penalties.

Where the engines share more than one tank, the fuel draws and returns are directed with a manifold — a set of valves — that should be clearly labeled. If such a manifold is fitted, to avoid overfilling a tank with return fuel, set the valves so each engine returns its excess fuel to the tank it is drawing from.

On a charter boat, make sure your onboard briefing includes a thorough demonstration of the fuel system.

If the fuel tanks are located in the hulls, monitor them to keep the fuel levels even to balance the weight in each hull.

A catamaran's engines are very often installed aft of the accommodations and accessed through deck hatches.

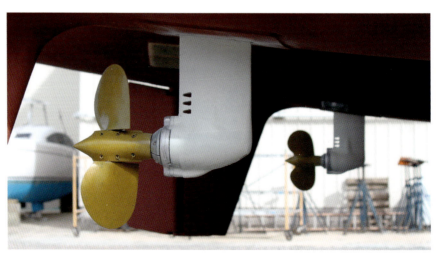

Saildrives are commonly used in catamarans. They eliminate the stern tube and stern gland needed with a propeller shaft but are installed through big holes in the hulls sealed with gaskets. Water for cooling the engine is drawn in through the drive leg.

[handwritten notes at top of page:]
DC = Edison — one direction / solar, ev — stable
AC = Tesla — change direction w/ transformers
· homes / businesses
→ easily increased / decreased — voltage can be stepped up or down to transfer over long distances more efficiently.

ELECTRICAL SYSTEMS

With more cabins, more heads, and two engines, cruising catamarans have complex electrical systems powered by multiple batteries. Some boats also have generators to deliver an AC supply similar to that in a home for powering high-draw appliances such as air conditioning and water heaters.

The most-used electrical circuits are usually controlled from a switch panel located in the boat's common area.

ELECTRICAL PANELS

Over the years, electrical systems on boats have undergone major changes. The control panels look different on newer boats — and there might be several of them. When chartering, make sure to get a thorough briefing on where the control panels are (for batteries, high DC loads, domestic DC circuits, and AC circuits) and how to operate them.

BATTERY CHARGING

[handwritten: AC: alternating (back, forth, bidirectional)]

When the boat is alongside a dock, the AC shorepower (either 110 or 220 volts, depending on your location) will provide ample power to run the AC appliances, incuding the battery charger. After departing the dock, unless you have a generator, you'll be dependent on the more limited 12-volt power supply from your batteries.

[handwritten: DC: direct current (battery)]

Two engines complicate the charging system. On most cruising catamarans, each start battery is collocated with an engine and is charged by the alternator

on that engine (or by the battery charger when AC power is available).

How you recharge the house batteries depends on the system installed by the builder. On some boats, only one engine is fitted with an alternator for charging the house batteries. In this arrangement, you'll have to run the so-called "master" engine more frequently than the other.

Should both engines have alternators fitted, you might have the choice of running either one for economy or both engines for a faster charge. Try to use the engines so their run hours accumulate evenly. They will then draw down their fuel tanks at the same rate and their maintenance schedules will be the same.

It's most important, for the safety, comfort, and happiness of the crew, that you verify exactly what charging system is employed on your boat and learn how to operate it. If you are chartering, be sure to get detailed instruction from your charter briefer.

If you have a generator on board, make sure your briefing includes a thorough demonstration of how to start it, engage it, and shut it down. While it's running, the generator will charge the batteries through the battery charger.

POWER MANAGEMENT

Manage your power usage to maintain a healthy charge in the house batteries. Avoid discharging them too deeply as recharging them will take a long time and, over the long term, frequent deep discharging will damage the batteries.

Some simple procedures, such as turning off lights and fans when you leave your cabin, will help to conserve power. On most boats, the refrigerator is

a major power eater, but a few easy steps will reduce the power usage. Ensure the fridge is turned to maximum when on shorepower or when the engine is running, and reduce the cooling level when you are sailing or at anchor. Keep the fridge full, open the door for the shortest time possible, and use a block of ice to help keep it cool.

Some boats are equipped with an inverter, which turns battery power into AC power. An inverter can power some AC appliances, but at a high cost to your 12-volt supply. A 900-watt coffee maker draws 7.5 amps at 120 volts AC — that's 75 amps from your 12-volt battery!

....

TIP *Monitor your house battery level. When the voltmeter reads 12.2 volts with no lights on or appliances running, it is at at 50 percent charge — time to recharge.*

....

Battery switches and circuit breakers for high-current DC circuits, such as the anchor windlass and electric winches, might be on a dedicated panel located near the batteries.

AC circuits, the generator start panel, and the generator/ shorepower selector switch will probably be on a control panel in a separate location from the DC circuits.

WATER SYSTEMS

All the water systems on a cruising catamaran — fresh, gray, toilet, and bilge — are the same as on a monohull. More hulls with more cabins, showers, and heads means more equipment and fittings to keep an eye on.

FRESH WATER

Water is delivered to faucets and showers under pressure. There might be a freshwater pump (and accumulator if needed) dedicated to each hull.

Where there are multiple water tanks, a manifold allows you to switch from one tank to the next. To maintain even weight distribution, try to keep the levels in freshwater tanks balanced, especially if they are large and located some distance away from the centerline of the boat, such as in the hulls.

Hot water is provided by a water heater that's plumbed off the engine's heat exchanger or an electric heating element when AC power is available from a generator or shore connection. On a charter boat, have your briefer describe the system. You'll certainly want to know which engine to run to make hot water.

Electrically operated marine toilets simplify the plumbing and the operating procedure.

....

TIP *Water is precious, so keep an ear open for a water pump that runs continuously, as that indicates an open faucet, an empty tank, or a freshwater leak.*

....

THE MARINE TOILET

On many cruising catamarans, instead of the traditional manual head, you are likely to encounter electric heads. The main difference from manual heads is the source of power for the pump. You measure the volume of water used by the length of time you hold the "flush" button. All the rules about what not to put in the toilet still apply! Follow the instructions to avoid problems.

GRAY AND BLACK WATER

Gray water from sinks and showers can be discharged overboard in most places. The discharge of black water (toilet sewage) is forbidden in many areas.

The freshwater system (red and blue tubing) becomes complex in two hulls. The pump with the gray tubing (for gray water) is a shower sump pump.

BILGE PUMPS

Two hulls means two bilges, and each requires its own bilge pumps. Each hull might have two electric bilge pumps, one for the engine compartment and one amidships. There should also be a manual bilge pump in each hull.

On some boats, the forward and aft compartments in the hulls are watertight, and connected with pipes to the main bilge. Valves on those pipes should remain closed except when draining water into the bilge so it can be pumped overboard.

Unless the showers drain into the bilge, there will be at least one gray-water sump pump in each hull.

The electric bilge pump discharges through a gray pipe. The other gray pipe is the manual bilge pump suction. The red-handled valves drain the fore and aft compartments.

When the galley on a catamaran is in the deckhouse it is blessed with an all-around view, and the cook can enjoy it while also taking part in the socializing.

GALLEY SYSTEMS

Although the galley on a cruising catamaran might be more spacious than on a comparable monohull, the equipment will be the same, just arranged somewhat differently.

APPLIANCES

The fridge and freezer could be separate units and access might be through doors on the front rather than lids in the top. If so, be aware that precious cold air will pour out whenever a door is opened — so don't stand in front of an open fridge door pondering what to take out.

Many galleys will be equipped with a microwave oven and electrical outlets for appliances like a blender, coffee pot, and toaster. Most of these devices will need shorepower or the generator. Before leaving the dock, make sure you know which, if any, AC appliances will run off the inverter (and when using them, bear in mind the effect on the batteries).

SAFETY PRECAUTIONS

While it's best to avoid preparing meals under way, the catamaran's level stance makes it easier than on a monohull. In a seaway, you might have to compensate for a quick and jerky motion, so it's still advisable to take precautions — like wearing foul-weather gear — to avoid burns and scalds. At anchor, a catamaran should not be sufficiently disturbed by swell or passing powerboats to make cooking hazardous.

Of course, the same precautions and procedures apply to the use of a propane stove as on any boat. Make sure the gas supply is turned off at the tank whenever the stove is not in use.

STOWING PROVISIONS

Overloading in general has a negative effect on performance, and catamarans are also sensitive to how and where heavy items are stowed. Due to the wide separation of the hulls, a difference in weight between hulls, as when water or fuel tanks are unevenly filled, will cause a small but noticeable *list* (the boat will lean to one side) when the boat is at rest. Performance will differ slightly on one tack from the other.

When stowing provisions, try to distribute heavier items, like canned goods and cases of beverages, equally between the hulls and place them as low as possible. Also, keep them close to amidships, as putting too much weight forward could lead to a bow-down attitude, which is undesirable when sailing fast downwind in heavy conditions. The pendulum effect of heavy bows can lead to more pronounced hobbyhorsing when sailing or motoring into a head sea.

CRUISING SAILBOAT SYSTEMS: REVIEW

Although sometimes more complex, the systems on a cruising catamaran are basically the same as covered in the ASA104 standard. The topics presented on this page are essentially a refresher of some of the more important procedures to remember.

ENGINES

A good habit to get into is to perform some basic engine checks every day before starting the engines.

■ **Lubrication:** Use the dipstick to check the engines' oil levels.

■ **Cooling systems:** Check that the raw-water seacocks are open for use and that the raw-water strainers are clean so that the engines' cooling water can run freely. Check the level of the coolant in the expansion tanks.

■ **Belts:** Test the tension of each alternator belt. Push on the belt. There should be no more than one inch of movement or the belt will slip. Check also for excessive dust (a sign of belt slip) and cracks.

■ **Miscellaneous:** Look around the engine compartments for loose or chafed wires, cracked hoses, leaking fluids, and any other sign that anything is amiss.

When you have done your pre-start checks, start the engines according to the required procedure. (When chartering, make sure to go through the starting procedure — including putting the battery switches on their correct settings — with your briefer, as the required steps can vary between engines from different manufacturers).

Before starting any engine, remember to put the gearshift in neutral.

High on the maintenance checklist for an engine are the coolant reservoir, raw-water strainer, and fuel filter.

Once an engine has started, look at the exhaust discharge. To prevent it from overheating, shut down an engine if no water is exiting with the exhaust. Check that other gauges and lights, such as those for water temperature and oil pressure, are functioning.

PROPANE STOVE

The propane stove is both efficient and simple to operate, but propane can be dangerous if mishandled. Everyone aboard who might use the stove must be shown how to use it properly and how to operate the propane system.

Propane is stored in cylinders, which are fitted in a dedicated locker designed to prevent the gas from entering the boat should a leak occur. To prevent gas from leaking into the boat, the valve on the top of the propane cylinder must remain closed except while the galley stove is in use. A regulator attached to the cylinder reduces the pressure of the gas before it enters the supply line into the boat. Inside the propane locker, a solenoid shut-off valve fitted on the low-pressure side of the regulator is operated by a switch located near the stove.

Be sure to follow the operating sequence for safely using the stove:

① Check the burner knobs are all "Off."

② Open the valve on the propane tank.

③ Turn the solenoid switch "On."

④ Select a burner knob, turn it to the "Light" position and push it in.

⑤ Light the burner, hold the knob in for several seconds, then release it.

⑥ Use the stove.

⑦ When finished, turn off the solenoid switch first and let the remaining gas in the line burn off.

⑧ Turn the burner knobs to "Off."

⑨ Close the valve on the propane tank.

HEAD TROUBLESHOOTING

If water doesn't pump into the bowl, check that the intake seacock is open.

If flushing becomes very difficult, stop pumping — the holding tank might be full and you might end up forcing the sewage out of the tank's vent.

With an electric toilet, you might not get the same indication that the holding tank is full (pumping resistance) as with a manual toilet. You might have to visually monitor the water level in the tank.

On a charter boat, it is best to call the charter base for assistance.

Each engine on a catamaran can be started, monitored, and shut down with its own control panel.

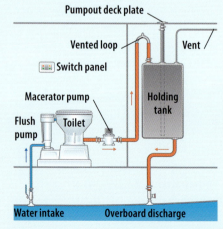

A typical electric toilet has two pumps. The holding tank can be pumped out or drained via the through-hull.

DECK HARDWARE: REVIEW

As you progressed through the ASA courses, from ASA101 Basic Keelboat to ASA104 Bareboat Cruising, you became familiar with winches and other hardware used when setting and trimming sails. On catamarans, while the hardware is essentially the same, you must respect the fact that you'll be handling greater forces.

WINCHES

On a cruising catamaran, do not attempt to hand-trim the sails even in light winds. You need the larger winches, and more wraps around the winches, to give you the power to safely control the sails.

When grinding a winch, use your upper-body strength, not just your arms. Make sure the handle is securely locked into the winch. When a line is heavily loaded, get your body over the winch, use both hands on the handle, and grind steadily, even if it feels slow, to conserve your energy.

A catamaran's size leads to some jobs requiring two people: one to grind and one to watch the results.

Place enough wraps of line on the winch that you can keep hold of the tail when it's time to ease the line. Make sure the tail is secure in the self tailer.

TIP *When in doubt, add a wrap — it's easy to take off an extra wrap but very hard to add one when you have too few.*

ROPE CLUTCHES

A rope clutch has an open position and a closed position. When open, it allows a line to pass freely in either direction. When locked closed, the clutch holds the line fast, preventing it from being eased (and from pulling against you) but still allowing it to be trimmed. Labeling rope clutches with the names of the lines they control helps the crew work with confidence when easing and trimming.

SAFETY TIP *Do not open a rope clutch that's carrying a line under load. If it is released too fast, the loaded line will be sure to injure you. First, take three or four turns around a winch. Take up the load by grinding the winch, then open the clutch and carefully ease the line off the winch.*

ELECTRIC WINCHES

Many catamarans are fitted with electric winches but you must always be aware of how powerful they are and always use them with great care.

If, when manually grinding a winch, you encounter unusual resistance, you stop and look for the reason. An electric winch will just keep on grinding, and can easily cause damage. Always watch what the winch is grinding, and keep fingers, hair, and clothing well clear of it.

Bear in mind, too, that, overusing electric winches can deplete your battery bank.

JIBSHEET CARS

The fairleads for the jibsheets are cars that slide on tracks fitted, usually, on the roof of the deckhouse. The cars can be locked into place on the track, and the position of a fairlead can be adjusted by disengaging the lock and moving the car forward or aft along the track.

Never attempt to move the fairlead car when it's under load from the jibsheet. Make your adjustment to the lazy (windward) car so it will be in the correct position when you tack.

When easing a line off a winch, squeeze the wraps on the drum to increase friction.

Make sure to open a rope clutch all the way when releasing a line and close it firmly when locking it.

To move the jibsheet car, lift the button to disengage the plunger that locks the car to the track.

REVIEW QUESTIONS (see page 90 for answers)

FILL IN THE BLANK

1 A Tripod rig refers to the arrangement of a forestay and _shrouds_ that support the mast without the need for a _backstay_ .

2 A forward projection of the bridgedeck designed to soften the impact of the seas is called a _needle_ .

3 On catamarans without fixed keels, a _daggerboard_ slides vertically through a trunk in each hull to provide lateral resistance and improved performance when sailing to _windward_ .

4 A catamaran's _stability_ is derived from the buoyancy in its two widely separated hulls. Even so, care must be taken to avoid overloading, and to distribute weight _evenly_ .

5 Located on the forward crossbeam, the _seagull_ _striker_ provides reinforcement to counter the effect of forestay tension.

6 The downward force of the catamaran's mast is supported by the center _crossbeam_ integrated into the bridgedeck structure. The mainsheet traveler is often mounted over the _aft_ crossbeam.

7 A typical cruising catamaran sail plan consists of a large _fully_ - _battened_ mainsail and a roller-furling jib.

8 When a catamaran's steering wheel is turned, the _rudders_ operate together because they are connected by a tie rod. They are smaller than those on a monohull, but their efficiency is increased due to the lack of _heeling_ .

9 Name four systems or components that must be duplicated on a catamaran: _engine_ , _running gear_ , _cooling_ , _exhaust_ .

10 An engine's _start_ battery is generally collocated with that engine and charged by an _alternator_ on the same engine.

11 Take care to ensure that levels in the _fuel_ and _freshwater_ tanks are balanced, especially if they are located away from the boat's centerline.

12 Less heeling makes preparing meals easier on a catamaran than on a monohull, but it's still advisable to take _precautions_ to avoid burns and _scalds_ .

For questions 13 and 14, identify the named parts with the lettered items in the diagram.

13 Cruising catamaran structure

- D ☐ Seagull striker
- b ☐ Ramp/catwalk
- g ☐ Trampoline
- f ☐ Bridgedeck
- A ☐ Forward crossbeam
- C ☐ Deckhouse
- E ☐ Keel

14 Catamaran rig

- i ☐ Diamond stays
- K ☐ Spreader/strut
- L ☐ Mainsheet traveler
- H ☐ Forestay
- J ☐ Topping lift

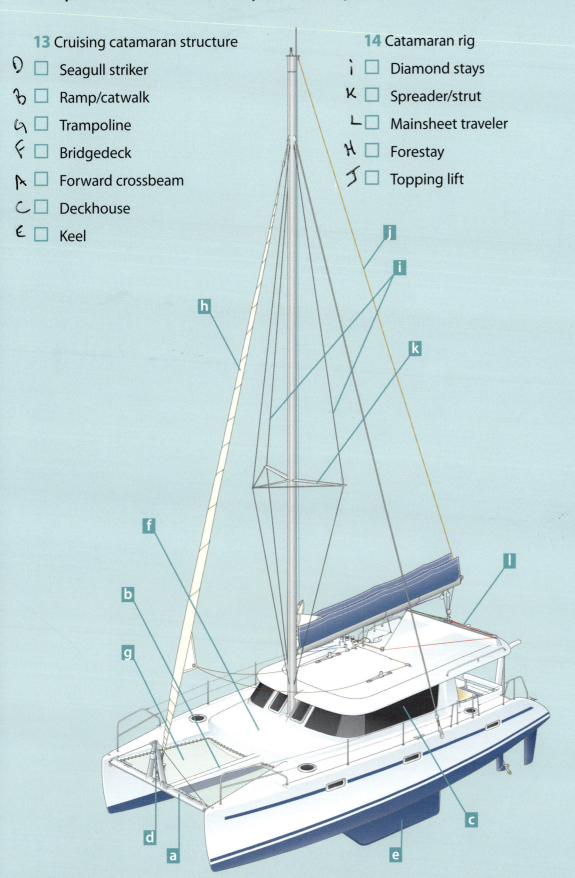

CHAPTER 3

Sailing a cruising catamaran

"Sailing is sailing" and the same principles and techniques apply on all boats that harness the power of the wind with sails. If you have come up through the ASA educational system, you have learned the theory and practice of sailing and seamanship. Now, aboard a cruising catamaran, you will be able to apply your skills directly to sailing this boat.

You will quickly discover that the sailing characteristics of a boat with lots of windage and two long, narrow hulls set quite far apart will, in certain conditions and situations, be very different from those of a monohull. In this chapter we will examine these differences and introduce some valuable techniques for getting the best performance out of a cruising catamaran.

Welcome to the world of catamaran sailing — have fun!

SAILING CHARACTERISTICS

Catamarans excel when reaching — sailing across the wind — and even a very cushy and relatively heavy cruising catamaran can outpace cruising monohulls of a comparable size on these points of sail. However, on upwind and dead-downwind courses, the compromises made to enhance cruising comfort — wider hulls, luxury appliances, and plush furnishings — affect the boat's performance.

THE CATAMARAN SAIL PLAN

Most cruising catamarans have a fractional rig with the sail area typically divided between a very large mainsail with a pronounced roach and a relatively small jib on a roller furler. For extra power when reaching in lighter winds, many privately owned cruising catamarans are rigged to set an asymmetrical spinnaker off a short bowsprit that projects from the forward crossbeam.

MAINSAIL

To safely clear the deckhouse and helm station, the boom and the mainsail must be high off the water. Adding sail area in the roach keeps the mainsail's center of effort (CE) low. This is preferable to making the sail (and the mast) taller, which would elevate the CE and add weight high up. The result is the large, full-battened mainsail with its massive roach, arguably one of the best sailing features of the cruising catamaran. For ease of furling, lazy-jacks guide the sail into a stack-pack cover on the boom.

This powerful and efficient sail, in combination with the catamaran's inherent stability, can generate high sailing speeds. However, it must be reefed early as the wind builds if the boat is not to become overpowered.

As sail engineering continues to evolve, more boats, including cruising catamarans, are using a "high-aspect-ratio" mainsail with a "square top." This more efficient sail allows the mast to be stepped farther aft without giving up much sail area while making room forward for a large self-tacking jib.

The large mainsail has a tendency to act as a weather vane, creating weather helm and causing the boat to want to turn toward the wind when sailing close-hauled. The effect is most noticeable at low speeds and when tacking. While the weather vane effect helps to bring the catamaran's bows into the tack, it can also hold the boat in irons. This can be avoided with use of a good tacking technique as described on page 47.

A broad roach supported by full-length battens puts lots of area in a mainsail with a relatively low CE, which is important on a cruising catamaran with its tall superstructure.

The square-top mainsail is more efficient than the "pin head." Another beneficial attribute is its ability to twist off and de-power the top of the sail in gusts.

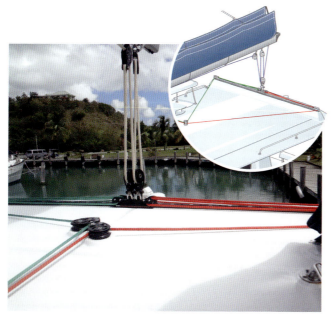

A long mainsheet traveler, made possible by a catamaran's wide beam, allows precise control of the mainsail's angle of attack. The mainsheet is used to control twist.

Not all catamarans are fitted with travelers. In a system with two separate mainsheets, the windward sheet controls the angle of attack and the leeward sheet controls twist.

MAINSHEET AND TRAVELER

For good trim, a mainsail with a large roach requires substantial mainsheet tension, as the leech twists off easily when the sheet is eased. This makes the mainsheet traveler (when one is fitted) an important tool for trimming the mainsail. On many cats, the traveler spans the full width of the bridgedeck (or the rigid cockpit roof), and it is long enough to be used to set the mainsail's angle of attack on all points of sail. The mainsheet is used primarily to adjust twist. A long traveler makes a boom vang unnecessary.

For broad reaching, set the traveler all the way to leeward, then adjust the mainsheet to achieve optimal trim and twist. While it's not a jibe preventer, if the car is secured to leeward, the long traveler can help mitigate the effects of an accidental jibe. By keeping the mainsheet short, it limits the arc the boom can swing through.

If your catamaran does not have a mainsheet traveler, it probably has two independent mainsheets. Both sheets are attached to the boom, with one led to a fixed point to starboard and the other to port. With this rig, use the windward sheet to set the angle of attack and the leeward sheet to control twist. A boom vang might be fitted to allow more control of twist when broad reaching.

THE MAINSAIL HALYARD

Due to its size, and the weight of the battens and the friction in the batten car system, a catamaran mainsail is heavy to hoist. To make it easier, the halyard is often rigged with a block at the head of the sail to provide a 2:1 purchase. (The same system is used on large monohulls.) This means you have to pull twice as much halyard tail to raise the sail. Crew jumping the halyard at the mast (backed up by someone taking up the slack at the winch) will speed up the process considerably, up to the point you need to crank the winch.

A downside of the 2:1 halyard is that you also have twice as much halyard tail to contend with when lowering the sail. Before easing the halyard, remember to flake out the tail so it can run free and not create tangles that will jam in a rope clutch or a block. Make sure also that it's not underfoot.

TOPPING LIFT

The topping lift has a big role, especially in the absence of a rigid boom vang. It should be eased, and then made fast again, after the sail is hoisted. Most important, it must be taken up before the sail is lowered so the boom doesn't fall onto the cockpit canopy. And don't forget to use it when reefing!

JIB

Catamaran jibs are generally small, and jibsheets are commonly led through cars on tracks inboard on the deckhouse roof where they give good sheeting angles for windward sailing. The sheets will be controlled by a winch on each side of the cockpit or led to a single winch (possibly electric) at the helm station.

On some boats, the jib is self-tacking and trimmed with a single sheet and a traveler on the foredeck.

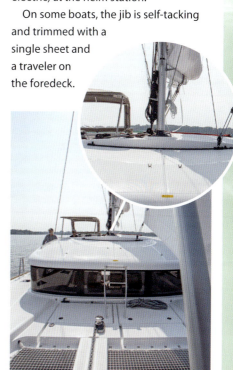

A self-tacking jib does not need to be tended when tacking the boat, but the sheet must be adjusted for trim.

SAILING TO WINDWARD

A cruising catamaran's high profile creates windage that has a negative effect on boat speed when sailing to windward. In big sea conditions, wave slam on the underside of the deck slows progress, as do the plunging bows as the boat hobbyhorses over the waves. Catamarans with shoal-draft keels are much more prone to leeway than deep-draft monohulls. Due to these factors, cruising catamarans go to windward best when sailed at a wider angle to the wind than monohulls — but faster.

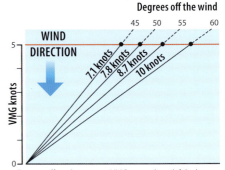

Footing off might increase VMG to windward if the boat gains enough speed. To achieve the same VMG at 55° to the true wind as at 45°, it must sail 23 percent faster.

CLOSE-HAULED SAIL TRIM

When sailing to windward on a catamaran, don't try to point too high. Begin on a close reach to build speed, then head up in small increments, trimming the sails as you do so, as you would on any boat.

To trim the mainsail, position the boom with the traveler to get the lower telltales streaming (if the sail has them) and then trim the mainsheet for optimum twist with the upper telltales streaming. You need more twist aloft in light winds than in moderate winds.

To trim the jib, set the angle of attack with the sheet and adjust foot depth and twist through lead position. You won't be able to adjust the lead position with the sheet loaded, so make your adjustment to the lazy sheet lead, then tack to test it.

In stronger winds, to de-power the top of the jib, increase twist by moving the jibsheet lead cars aft.

Watch the apparent wind speed. Be ready to head up or ease the mainsheet (or the traveler if that's easier) to de-power the mainsail in gusts. Reef early rather than too late (see page 52).

VMG TO WINDWARD

Every boat has its optimal combination of true-wind angle and boat speed for best velocity made good (VMG) to windward in different wind strengths and sea conditions. If you try to point too high (pinch) before attaining optimum upwind speed, you will end up slipping to leeward and making poor windward progress. This effect is pronounced on many cruising cats due to their shoal draft and high windage. You can't expect a cat to point as high as a monohull, so foot off and sail faster.

Be aware, though, that footing off too much hurts VMG unless the speed increase is significant, as the diagram above shows. To find the sweet spot where your cruising catamaran makes its best VMG, note your boat speed while sailing on different true wind angles.

CLOSE REACHING

When you bear away to a close reach, ease the traveler to leeward until the mainsail begins to luff, then haul it back up a touch to stop the luff. With a two-sheet arrangement, ease the windward sheet and adjust the leeward sheet to set the twist.

Good sail trim on any boat, cat or mono, can be judged by evenly streaming telltales on the jib and a mainsail that luffs evenly when the traveler is eased to leeward. Use the masthead fly, if the boat has one, to check the apparent wind angle.

TIP *Check your rudder angle either with the autopilot display or the position of the steering wheel to see if your sails are balanced. If you have weather helm, it's probably due to an over-trimmed mainsail.*

TACKING

With two long, slender hulls set far apart, a catamaran is inherently resistant to turning. Both hulls lose speed in a turn, the "inside" hull more than the outer, and the tighter the turn the greater the loss of speed. Add small rudders and a large weather-vaning mainsail and tacking in some conditions becomes a challenge.

Follow the process described here and your crew should be able to tack comfortably in all but the lightest wind conditions. Practice will pay dividends.

① Going into the tack, you must have good boat speed and be sailing close-hauled and not on a reach. Wait for a smooth patch of water and . . .

② Turn the wheel steadily, not so far or so fast that the rudders stall or the boat slows excessively. Ease the jibsheet a little.

③ As the boat comes head to wind, don't release the jibsheet too early. If the boat seems to be slowing in its turn, delay releasing the "old" jibsheet and let the backwinded jib help to "blow" the bow out of irons and on to the new tack. If the boat seems to be coasting through the turn smoothly, you can release the jibsheet just as it starts to show signs of backwinding.

④ After the boat has turned past head to wind, keep the wheel over to complete the turn. Ease the traveler to leeward a few feet and/or ease the mainsheet a few

inches to reduce the mainsail's weather-vane effect. Trim the jib quickly to assist the turn and regain speed.

⑤ Let the boat turn beyond your new eventual close-hauled course and sail a little "wide," footing off while trimming the sails to build boat speed.

⑥ As boat speed builds, resume your optimum course to windward and trim the mainsheet and traveler back to their close-hauled positions.

TIP *Backwinding the jib slows the boat — but not as much as getting stuck in irons! Practice the timing of the jibsheet release and be sensitive to the power and control it can give you in the maneuver.*

IN IRONS

If you get into irons, be patient. Ease the mainsheet and tighten the jibsheet. If the boat gathers sternway, steer the stern to put the wind on one side of the bow. Trim the jib to build forward speed before trimming the mainsail.

As a last resort, use the "outside" engine to push you around.

WIND DIRECTION

⑥
⑤
④
③
②
①

APPARENT WIND

To achieve optimum sail trim and steer the boat for the best performance, all sailors need to understand and apply the concept of apparent wind. This is especially important for sailors on boats that accelerate rapidly in response to an increase in wind strength or a change in course, which is the case for many catamarans when reaching.

When sailing to windward and when reaching, an increase in boat speed yields an increase in the apparent wind speed and a decrease in the apparent wind angle (i.e., the apparent wind moves forward and strengthens). The sails might begin to luff, so you'll need to trim them tighter or bear away to keep them full. At some point, when sailing close-hauled, you can trim no further, and bearing away is the only option.

When sailing downwind on a run, an increase in boat speed causes the apparent wind speed to

decrease. Especially in light airs, all cruising boats can benefit from heading up slightly to a broad reach, where the apparent wind on the sails is stronger (and farther forward). This increases boat speed and results in better downwind VMG than sailing dead downwind (see page 50). You end up jibing between broad-reaching courses to reach the destination.

Cruising catamarans, with their slender hulls and faster reaching speeds, tend to respond very well to this technique, even as the wind gets stronger.

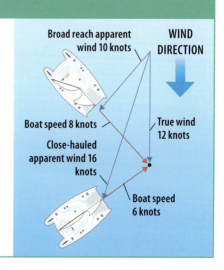

Broad reach apparent wind 10 knots

WIND DIRECTION

Boat speed 8 knots

True wind 12 knots

Close-hauled apparent wind 16 knots

Boat speed 6 knots

REACHING AND RUNNING

When reaching, the general rule of sail trim still applies: Once you are on your desired course, ease the sails until they begin to luff and then retrim them. However, on a deep broad reach or a run, the rule ceases to work as the sails are no longer functioning as airfoils; your best measure of trim is boat speed.

SAIL TRIM WHEN REACHING

As you bear away from a close reach you enter the region where a catamaran sails fastest. While boat speed will increase significantly, the apparent wind angle will remain quite tight and the jibsheet and mainsheet traveler won't have to be eased as much as on a slower cruising monohull on the same point of sail.

As the boat accelerates, the apparent wind speed will increase. Taking in a reef might be prudent if the wind strength is already on the high side (see page 52).

BEAM REACHING

A catamaran truly comes alive when beam reaching. Due to the high sailing speed, when the true wind is on the beam, the apparent wind is forward of the beam. The seas are on the beam, resulting in an exhilarating ride with a fairly easy motion.

Find the best mainsail trim by playing the traveler and mainsheet. To obtain the best jib trim, you'll need to move the jibsheet lead forward so you can control twist by pulling down on the leech.

BROAD REACHING

Due to the catamaran's preferred sailing angles, whenever your destination is downwind you'll spend most of your time broad reaching. Set the mainsail's angle of attack by easing the traveler to leeward and use the mainsheet to control twist.

On a broad reach, jib trim can be challenging on a cruising catamaran. The jibsheet tracks are positioned well inboard on the deckhouse roof to create a good sheeting angle for upwind sailing, but they are not well positioned for sheets eased for broad reaching. The solution, if the boat is suitably equipped, is to rig a Barber-hauler: Attach a second sheet and lead it outboard to a block attached near the toerail, where it will allow better control of the twist.

JIBING

Jibing a catamaran is less difficult than tacking as it's much easier to maintain speed through the maneuver. You must, however, keep the large mainsail under control as it crosses over the boat.

To prepare for the jibe, center the mainsheet traveler. Wrap the leeward control line several times around its winch and make fast both control lines. Ease the mainsheet a little so the sail isn't overtrimmed. To prevent the jib from wrapping around the forestay, take up all the slack on the lazy jibsheet.

Turn slowly downwind and haul in on the mainsheet to center the boom. As soon as the mainsail has jibed, ease the mainsheet and stop the turn so the boat doesn't continue to round up.

Ease the old leeward, now windward, traveler control line so the car can slide to leeward. After the jibe, haul the car all the way to leeward and make the new leeward control line fast. Retrim the mainsail and the jib for the new course.

On a catamaran without a traveler, ease the leeward sheet while using the windward sheet to center the mainsail. After the mainsail jibes over, ease both sheets, then adjust them both to trim the sail for your new course.

When broad reaching in moderate winds, the apparent wind is near the beam, so the boom does not need to be eased beyond the end of the traveler. On this double-mainsheet boat, the leeward sheet acts like a vang/preventer.

RUNNING

Sailing on a run is rarely the best choice on a catamaran. The jib fills easily sailing wing on wing on a boat that doesn't roll, but the chance of the wind getting on the wrong side of the big mainsail is increased because the tripod rig limits how far the boom can be eased forward. Catamarans in general make their best VMG toward a downwind destination when jibed from a broad reach on one tack to a broad reach on the opposite tack, taking advantage of the effect of boat speed on the apparent wind. When running does offer the best course, such as in a narrow channel that would otherwise require many and frequent jibes, use a preventer on the boom.

PREVENTER

When the mainsheet traveler has been hauled all the way to leeward and secured, a preventer is not normally needed — and some skippers never use one. However, in light air and a big sea, a

When sailing downwind or broad reaching on a catamaran, the boom is rarely eased very far beyond the end of the traveler. Even so, a preventer led from the end of the boom to the bow will steady the sail in a seaway.

preventer can steady the boom and help keep the mainsail drawing, even on a broad reach. A strong line led forward from the end of the boom to a suitably strong deck fitting, like a mooring cleat amidships or forward, will do the job.

DAGGERBOARDS

Catamarans designed for higher performance are usually fitted with daggerboards. They impart markedly better upwind sailing qualities — by reducing leeway — and can also be used to help balance the helm.

For optimum performance when sailing upwind or reaching in light to moderate winds, the leeward board should be fully down. (Many sailors leave just one or even both boards down rather than raise one and lower the other when tacking).

In stronger winds, less board is needed. At the higher boat speeds achieved when reaching in strong winds, the boards should be fully retracted so neither they or their trunks suffer damage from excessive hydrodynamic pressure.

When sailing downwind, retract the boards to reduce drag and turbulence, although you may find a little board down improves the steering on some catamarans.

In extreme conditions, both boards should be up.

In shallow waters, raise the boards to avoid grounding. A hard grounding could damage a board and its trunk, which could lead to flooding.

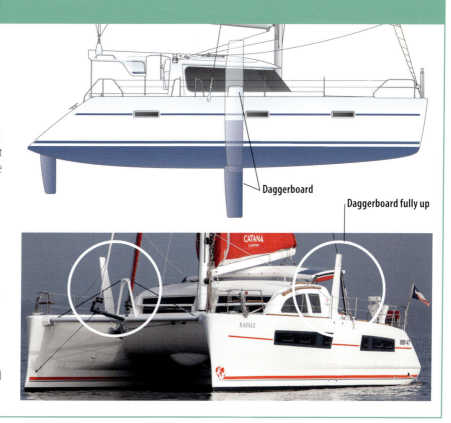

Daggerboard

Daggerboard fully up

DOWNWIND SAILING TACTICS

Sailors quickly learn the concepts of the no-sail zone and tacking to reach an upwind destination. Since any boat can sail downwind, it's more difficult to accept the idea that sailing directly toward a downwind destination might not be the fastest way to get there.

DOWNWIND VMG

Most sailboats, in all but very strong winds, sail faster on a broad reach than a run. Exploiting this faster reaching speed can often result in higher downwind VMG. This is especially the case with catamarans because of their inherent ability to achieve high sailing speeds.

The illustration below shows a case in which a catamaran crew plans to sail from Spanish Town to Road Harbour in the British Virgin Islands on a day the direct course, or rhumb line, is dead downwind.

It would be possible to sail that course wing on wing (boat A), but by setting off on the port tack and sailing high enough for the jib to fill, boat B will sail faster and under more control. If the wind backs toward north, it will have the option to head up away from the land or to jibe onto starboard tack and reach toward Road Harbour. If the wind veers toward south, it can bear away and reach directly toward Road Harbour without jibing.

Assuming the wind stays constant, boat B, sailing 20 degrees above the direct course, only needs to sail slightly faster — by less than .5 knot — to have a higher VMG than boat A's 6 knots. Sailing at 7 knots its VMG is superior.

Sailing higher yet might improve the VMG further, but there is a limit. Boat C, while sailing much faster, is not achieving the same downwind VMG as boat B.

At some point, a jibe will be needed to bring the boat to its destination. Figuring out when that must be is a good exercise in piloting.

This is the simplest case, where wind direction is aligned with the course, but any time you are sailing to a downwind destination, finding your optimum course for best downwind VMG will get you there fastest. In all other cases, just as when sailing to windward, start out by sailing on your favored tack. That's the one on which your bow points closer to your destination.

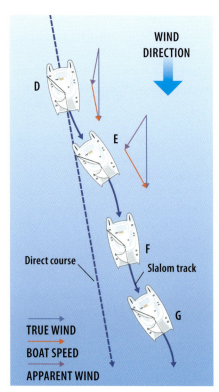

Sail a slalom to find the course for best downwind VMG. Head up a few degrees to bring the apparent wind forward and increase boat speed, then bear away a little.

SEEKING VMG

Most cruising sailors don't want to be constantly adjusting sail trim while sailing downwind. Fortunately, it's possible to achieve good VMG downwind without fussing a lot with the sails. You'll end up steering a "slalom" course.

① Start by sailing on a broad reach, sails properly trimmed, but with the jib on the edge of being blanketed by the mainsail (Boat D). Note your course and boat speed and calculate your VMG.

② Head up a few degrees toward a beam reach, to bring the apparent wind forward (boat E), and trim accordingly. This will increase your boat speed and bring the apparent wind forward even more. Note your speed, course, and VMG.

③ Carrying that speed, head down a few degrees toward a broad reach (boat F).

④ As your speed drops, head up again to increase boat speed (boat G). Again, note your speed, course, and VMG.

⑤ After a little slaloming, you will find your groove for best downwind VMG.

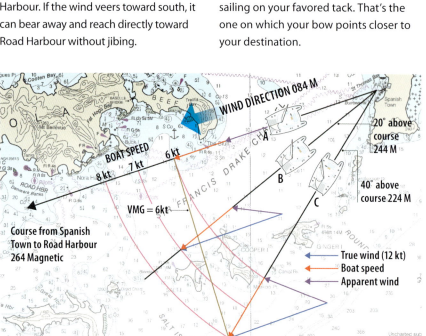

In light to moderate winds, broad reaching can lead to higher boat speeds and better VMG than sailing dead downwind.

CATAMARAN SKILLS PRACTICE

If you learned basic sailing on a monohull, you will find a catamaran feels and handles differently under sail and under power. Your ASA114 instructor will show you ways to get the best (and safest) performance out of the boat, but nothing teaches better than practice. Hone your skills by practicing some of these maneuvers in moderate winds.

FIGURE EIGHTS

Tacking a catamaran is sometimes challenging to sailors accustomed to the snappy response of a keelboat. Sailing a catamaran around a figure-eight course will give you lots of tacking practice.

- Build up good boat speed before tacking and initiate the tack from a close-hauled course.
- After tacking, trim the sails for a close-reach course to build speed.
- Continue the turn to a beam reach.
- Ease the sails and bear away to a broad reach to get downwind of the next mark.
- Gradually head up toward a close-hauled course, trimming the sails as you go.
- Tack and repeat.
- You can also sail a figure eight by jibing around each mark.

OVALS

Sailing a catamaran around an oval course will have you alternately tacking and jibing, which is good training for crew coordination. The oval course gives you more flexibility with your turning marks relative to the wind . . . they don't necessarily have to be in line with the wind or perpendicular to it.

PRACTICE REEFING

Before you have to reef in earnest, you should know each step of the procedure (see page 52). That means also learning where all the reefing lines are, which rope clutches and winches control them, and the sequence of steps to follow.

On a calm day, practice reefing at the dock. On the water, practice reefing in light winds so you can "learn the ropes" without the stress that high winds bring.

HEAVE-TO

Practice heaving-to, as it might be a very different experience on a catamaran than

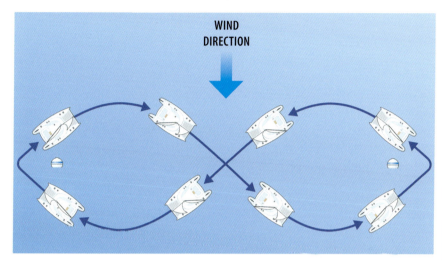

To practice sailing a figure-eight course, find a pair of marks that lie across the wind (or use one mark and an imaginary mark). Don't have them too close together — you'll need time between tacks to pick up speed.

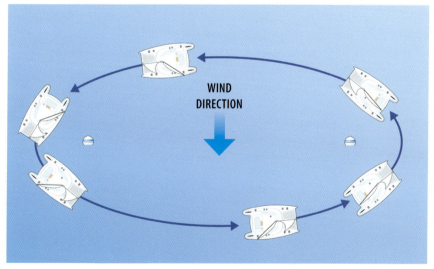

By sailing an oval course, you can practice tacking and jibing alternately. The orientation of your course to the wind is not critical . . . if the course is not perpendicular to the wind, you'll simply sail a parallelogram.

on a cruising monohull. From a close-hauled course, tack and leave the jib sheeted in. After tacking, adjust the mainsail with the traveler (or the two mainsheets) and the rudders to hold the boat at the desired angle to the wind.

Use your tacking practice to help you tack successfully into your hove-to position. Try first in light air, then build on your technique in stronger winds.

MAN OVERBOARD RECOVERY

Practice MOB maneuvers. Figure out the best technique for your boat by trying the methods described on pages 72-73 and seeing how your boat responds. Practice return maneuvers from every point of sail and also practice with the engines, as you will probably have to use them.

Remember, don't practice your MOB drills with a live "victim."

HEAVY-WEATHER TACTICS

How you deal with heavy weather depends to some extent on how long you expect it to last — is it a passing squall, a large thunderstorm, or a building gale? In some situations, reefing just isn't enough to handle extremely strong winds. At this point — or long before if you've been paying attention to the weather — you should be looking for a safe harbor you can reach with the least difficulty.

WHEN TO REEF

One of the important aspects of sailing a cruising catamaran is that, because of the minimal heeling, the boat gives less of a sensory signal when it's time to reef the sails. You have to be especially wary about the effects of strengthening winds. As the wind increases, the boat will accelerate, increasing the apparent wind and making the need to reef more urgent.

Indications that it's time to reef and reduce the sail forces and rig loading are slack leeward shrouds and the leeward hull much more deeply immersed than the windward hull. Keep an eye on the leeward bow and on the wakes. A much bigger leeward wake than windward wake might mean you are overpowered.

Catamaran builders provide charts that specify wind speeds at which each reef must be taken to ensure the boat is carrying a safe amount of sail. Ensure that you have this chart on board before you leave the dock. To be safe, treat the builder's speed numbers as the **higher** of apparent wind or true wind, whichever is the case on the course you are sailing.

REEFING STEP BY STEP

Reefing follows the same procedure on a catamaran as on a monohull, and is best done when sailing on a close reach with the jib driving the boat.

① Turn to a close reach and trim the jib to maintain boat speed.

② Ease the traveler and mainsheet to completely luff the main. Ease the boom vang if the boat has one. Take up and secure the topping lift.

③ Ease the halyard to lower the mainsail until the reefing tack is at the gooseneck.

④ Tension the new tack with the reefing line (or place the reef cringle on its hook).

⑤ Re-tension the halyard.

⑥ Tension the clew reefing line. Bring the clew close to the boom but try to avoid pinching the sailcloth or battens under the reefing line.

⑦ Ease the topping lift.

⑧ Resume your desired course and trim the mainsail and jib appropriately.

NOTE Pay especially close attention to building wind and seas when you are sailing off the wind. Reef early, and use caution as you turn up to a close reach to

reef. As you do so, the apparent wind will increase significantly, as will the effect of the waves. Don't sheet in the mainsail; use the jib for power. When you turn downwind after reefing, be ready to ease the traveler and the jibsheet.

The critical moment in both these maneuvers is when you are beam-on to the waves. Ease the mainsail and let the jib drive the boat through the turn.

REEFING SEQUENCE

It's usual to reef the mainsail first to lower the center of effort. The next step might be to furl some of the jib, but read the reefing chart supplied by the catamaran's manufacturer or the charter company for specific guidance.

....
TIP *In stronger winds, head up into the gusts when sailing to windward and bear away in the gusts when sailing off the wind.*
....

WATCH WIND AND WAVES

Wind speed and angle are not the only indicators that it's time to reef — the sea

The object of reefing is to reduce the area of the sails and also to lower the center of effort. Doing both reduces the heeling moment as well as the wind force on the sails. Reefing the mainsail is usually the first step as it has the most effect on the center of teffort. The boat's operating manual will provide specific instructions for the best reefing sequence.

This catamaran is enjoying a romp in a stiff breeze in sheltered water. It's heeled a few degrees and the leeward wake is more pronounced than the windward wake. In waves created by the same wind on open water, it might be wise to reef.

state is also important. When waves are significant, initiate reefing sooner than you might in flatter seas. Beam seas would cause you to reef earlier, whereas in following seas with lesser wave heights the process could be left a little later.

Keep a weather eye to windward and be ready to reef as soon as you see a squall approaching — don't wait until it's on top of you.

MOTORSAILING

Motoring with the aid of a reefed mainsail can get you to windward more effectively in a strong wind than sailing under a reefed mainsail and a deeply furled jib. Use both engines so you don't have to use the rudders to compensate for a shifted pivot point, and adjust your course and speed to achieve the best VMG while keeping your mainsail full.

HEAVING-TO

Heaving-to is not only useful in heavy weather, it's also a way to "park" the boat to kill time. For example, you might want to wait for the tide to change so you won't be entering an inlet against a strong current. Practice heaving-to in fair weather to perfect your technique.

Most catamarans will heave-to quite comfortably with a partially furled jib and a double-reefed mainsail. If the boat wants to lie beam-on to the seas — a bad position for any boat in large or breaking seas — furling the jib might allow the mainsail to hold the boat more into the wind. You don't, though, want the boat

head-on to the waves and vulnerable to being pushed sternward against the rudders. Play the traveler and the mainsheet to point higher or point lower. Daggerboards should be raised to allow the boat to slip sideways.

Lying ahull under "bare poles" (with all sails lowered) is another tactic that can be used in moderate sea conditions (as in a local squall or thunderstorm). The boat will normally turn slightly downwind and drift at about 5 knots.

DOWNWIND TACTICS

Sailing fast is sometimes a good tactic if it allows you to "run off" downwind to avoid an approaching storm. However, at high downwind speeds, a catamaran can sometimes travel faster than the waves. This puts it at risk of burying its bows and broaching or, in a worst case, pitchpoling stern over bow.

Slow the boat down by reefing so that it is not overtaking the waves and the rudders can maintain positive steering. In extreme circumstances, take down all the sails. In conditions that warrant this, a catamaran will travel fast enough to be steered downwind under bare poles.

Reefing is not just a tactic for persistent heavy weather. When the wind is gusty, reef the main[ ] they are the right size for the heavier gusts. Unfurl some headsail if you want more power in [ ]

CHAPTER 4

A catamaran under power

Many sailors are attracted to catamarans because they offer exhilarating sailing speeds, spacious decks and living quarters, and a stable ride. A feature that's not so apparent until you're actually on board and operating a catamaran is its phenomenal maneuverability under power at low speeds. Two engines and two propellers spaced widely apart enable you to pivot a catamaran 360 degrees within its own length — in either direction — without touching the steering wheel.

While you won't want to spend your sailing day pirouetting your catamaran, you'll certainly appreciate this maneuverability when docking, anchoring, or even hoisting sails. Operating a twin-engine catamaran under power is very different from operating a single-engine monohull, so you'll want to take a little time to learn the nuances and practice the new skills — and yes, maybe do a little showboating.

MANEUVERING UNDER POWER

In powerboat lingo, twin engines and twin propellers are known as "twin screws," but on a catamaran, you have twin screws on steroids. Those two propellers, one beneath each hull, are far enough apart that, operated singly or together, they can efficiently turn the boat in a very tight space. You can use this leverage to your advantage, especially when maneuvering in close quarters.

PROPELLER VARIATIONS

Propeller arrangements affect how a boat handles in subtle ways. Propellers on conventional shafts, which usually angle downward a little, will create some degree of prop walk. Propellers on saildrive units exhibit little or no prop walk.

On most monohull twin-screw powerboats, the port and starboard propellers rotate in opposite directions (counter-rotating), which nullifies prop-walk effects. On many catamarans they rotate in the same direction, but they are far enough apart that any prop-walk effect can be overcome by using the throttles to manipulate the thrust exerted by each propeller. You might see a slight difference between turning to port and turning to starboard with propellers on angled shafts.

When the propellers are forward of the rudders and the engines are in forward gear, turning the rudders deflects the prop wash, which helps when making turns at low speed. In reverse gear, the prop wash has no affect on the rudders.

On some catamarans, saildrive units are installed aft of the rudders, which means there is no prop-wash effect on the rudders with the engines in forward gear. However, there is prop wash on the rudders in reverse gear. This makes it necessary to hold the helm firmly when an engine is in reverse gear. Steering at low speeds with this configuration is only possible with the use of *differential power*.

....

TIP *During an onboard charter briefing, ask about the propeller arrangement on your catamaran and get tips from your briefer on how it will affect maneuvering.*

....

DIFFERENTIAL POWER

At low speeds or when maneuvering, the wide spacing of the propellers on a catamaran conveys a big advantage. By applying differential power — more rpm to one propeller than the other — you can cause the boat to turn. With one engine in forward gear and the other in reverse, the effect is magnified.

STANDING TURN

From standing still, it's possible to turn a catamaran within its own "footprint." For this maneuver, center the rudders and secure the steering wheel.

■ Standing turn to starboard: At the same time, gently shift the port engine to forward gear and the starboard engine to reverse. Gradually increase the thrust equally on both engines.

■ Standing turn to port: At the same time, gently shift the starboard engine to forward gear and the port engine to reverse. Gradually increase the thrust equally on both engines.

In both these cases, the boat will rotate about its center if equal thrust is applied (which might not be equal rpm).
NOTE Equal thrust does not necessarily mean equal rpm. Few propellers deliver the same thrust at the same rpm in forward and reverse.

THE PIVOT POINT

The point around which the boat rotates when turning is called the *pivot point*. In a monohull it approximates to the hull's center of lateral resistance (CLR), which is usually near the center of the keel, and its position doesn't change much.

Each hull of a catamaran has its own CLR. In normal operating mode, with both engines in either forward or reverse gear at the same thrust, the pivot point is equidistant between the two hulls. It can, though, be made to change its postion.

When you apply differential power, the pivot point moves toward the hull with the lesser thrust on the propeller. This can be very handy when maneuvering into and out of docks.

The pivot point moves in a similar way when one engine is in forward gear and the other in reverse. This effect can be

Twin engines are operated independently. In this case, each engine has a single-lever control combining the gearshift and throttle. A center position is neutral. Pushing a lever forward engages forward gear; pulling back engages reverse gear.

seen when you perform a standing turn. When prop thrust is equal, the pivot point is in the center of the boat. When power is applied differentially, the pivot point moves toward the hull on which the lesser thrust is applied. When making a standing turn to starboard, applying more thrust with the port engine than the starboard engine will move the pivot point toward the starboard hull . . . and vice versa.

When maneuvering, it's important to know where the pivot point is and how it moves as the thrust is varied. However, except in the case of equal and opposite thrust, the pivot point is not the center of the boat's turning circle. The radius of that circle depends on the difference in thrust applied to each propeller, both in amount and direction.

MOTORING AT CRUISING SPEED

When you are motoring a catamaran from one place to another, the normal practice is to run both engines at equal rpm and steer with the wheel. At cruising speeds, the rudders are very effective. Coupled with the catamaran's directional stability, this allows the autopilot to steer without undue stress.

If you are not in a big hurry and want to save fuel, you can run just one engine. Diesel engines work better under higher loads than at idle, so running one engine at 60 percent power will be better for the engine than operating both engines at 30 percent. You will have to compensate with the helm to steer a straight course because of the lever arm between the operating prop and the boat's pivot point, which in this case will be on the centerline of the opposite hull.

Which engine you use might depend on how the boat's electrical system is set up. If you want to charge the batteries and only one engine does that, you don't have a choice. Otherwise, it's better to run each engine on alternate occasions to maintain equal running hours (and simplify maintenance schedules).

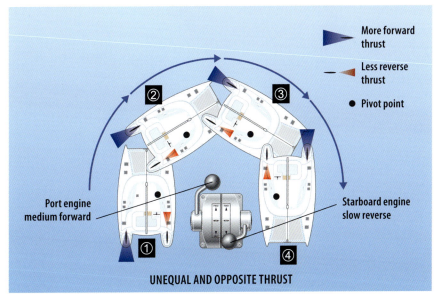

UNEQUAL AND OPPOSITE THRUST

LOOPING TURN: With unequal thrust in forward and reverse, the pivot point is toward the side on which the thrust is lower. Its location depends on the thrust differential between the two propellers, as does the radius of the induced turn.

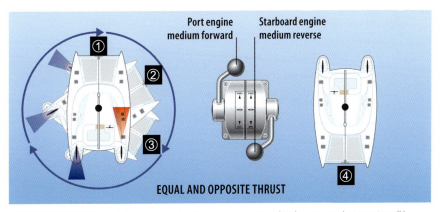

EQUAL AND OPPOSITE THRUST

STANDING TURN With equal thrust in forward and reverse on opposites sides, the catamaran's pivot point will be on its centerline. Trying this maneuver for the first time is an "oh, wow!" moment for newcomers to boats with twin screws.

MOVING FORWARD OR ASTERN - SHOPPING CART ANALOGY

When maneuvering a catamaran at slow speed in close quarters, center the wheel and use your propellers for turning. Think of it as pushing or pulling a shopping cart. Push or pull on the two throttles as you would do on opposite sides of the handle on the shopping cart.

■ **To turn clockwise:** Pull back the right hand (throttle); push forward the left hand.

■ **To turn counterclockwise:** Pull back the left hand (throttle); push forward the right hand.

SLOW-SPEED MANEUVERING

As you approach an area where you need to operate at a slower speed, like an anchorage or harbor, throttle back equally on the engines and continue to steer with the rudders. As the speed drops, the rudders become less effective, and you'll need to use differential power to assist with turning the boat.

■ Slow-speed turn to starboard: Turn the wheel to starboard. Reduce power on the starboard engine. Shift it to neutral and add power on the port engine if needed for a quicker turn.

■ Slow-speed turn to port: Turn the wheel to port. Reduce power on the port engine. Shift it to neutral and add power on the starboard engine if needed for a quicker turn.

■ Stop the boat: Easy does it! Throttle back both engines to idle and pause in neutral for a moment. Center the helm, take a firm grip on the wheel, then ease both levers into reverse. Gradually raise the rpm equally on both to take off forward motion smoothly.

When maneuvering with the engines, center the rudders and immobilize the steering wheel by leaning on it so the rudders cannot move. With one hand on each lever, make slow and deliberate gear changes and throttle adjustments.

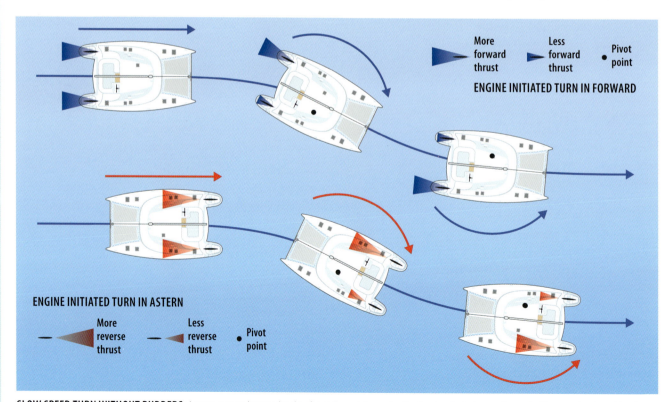

More forward thrust Less forward thrust • Pivot point

ENGINE INITIATED TURN IN FORWARD

ENGINE INITIATED TURN IN ASTERN

More reverse thrust Less reverse thrust • Pivot point

SLOW SPEED TURN WITHOUT RUDDERS: A catamaran can be turned at slow forward speeds by varying the thrust on the twin propellers and without turning the rudders (upper sequence). The same applies when motoring in astern (lower sequence), but the steering wheel must be restrained so the sternward movement cannot force the rudders to turn.

When motoring in astern, maintain a constant body position so you are less likely to become disoriented. So you have both hands free for operating the throttles, lean against the steering wheel to prevent the rudders from turning.

■ Back slowly to port: Center the wheel and maintain starboard reverse power. Reduce power on the port engine, or shift it to neutral or slow forward to increase the rate of turn.

■ Back slowly to starboard: Center the wheel and maintain port reverse power. Reduce power on the starboard engine, or shift it to neutral or slow forward to increase the rate of turn.

STATION KEEPING

You may find the need to hold a position — keep station — while waiting for a bridge to open or for your turn at a fuel dock. *Station keeping* is easily done with twin screws. Where there's no current, use the engines to hold the boat either bow or stern to the wind. In a current, hold the boat's bow between the current and the wind. Establish a range (two objects) or a bearing (one object) off the beam, and use small touches of port and starboard power as needed to hold your heading and maintain position relative to your range or bearing.

TIP The rudder angle indicator on the autopilot display will show you when the rudders are centered.

MOTORING IN ASTERN

With twin screws spaced well apart, you have excellent control in astern. For most maneuvers in astern, putting the throttle levers in the idle position, which is about 1,000 rpm on many engines, is sufficient. Even at idle speed, the boat may move too fast, in which case, ease the engines in and out of reverse gear as needed to maintain a safe speed.

■ Back in a straight line: Center and lock the wheel, then put both engines into reverse gear and raise the rpm of both equally. If prop walk seems to pull the stern to one side, counteract it by adjusting the rpm. The same applies in a crosswind, when you may be "crabbing" down a fairway and have to use a little differential power to stay in the middle.

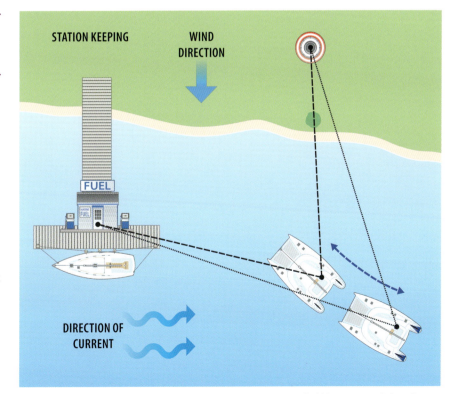

When station keeping, use ranges and/or bearings to verify the boat's position and hold that position with thrust from the engines as needed to counter the wind and current. If there is no current, hold the bow or stern directly into the wind.

DOCKING A CATAMARAN

As with docking any vessel, try to work with the elements rather than against them. Where you have a choice, avoid crosswind situations and motor into the wind or the current, whichever is dominant. Prepare your docklines well ahead of time. Place fenders strategically and use as many as you need to protect the straight, flat hulls.

USE THE PROPELLERS

When you're maneuvering around docks, the rudders will become less effective as your speed slows. This is where you use your twin screws to great advantage. Center the helm, and maneuver solely with the engines and propellers.

SIDE-TIE APPROACH

With twin screws, you have the ability to rotate the catamaran in either direction, so you can berth starboard-side-to or port-side-to with equal ease. The view from the helm station may dictate your preferred side, so that you can most

When planning an arrival at a dock, take into account the strength and direction of the wind and current, the dock structure, and the movements of nearby boats.

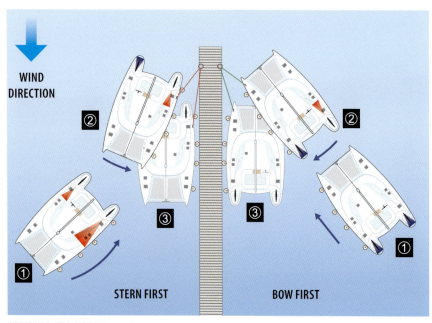

ARRIVING AT A SIDE TIE: Use the engines to steer the boat toward the dock and to work it alongside with the help of a dockline. Approaching stern first might be beneficial in some situations, especially if that gives you the better view.

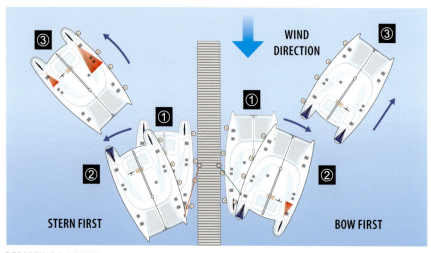

DEPARTING A SIDE TIE: Use the engines, spring lines, and the wind as appropriate to rotate the catamaran away from the dock so you can motor away in forward or reverse. Double the spring line so you can recover it from on board.

easily see your target. Depending on the wind direction or your view from the helm, you might also find it's to your advantage to approach stern first.

To work the boat into a berth against a crosswind, you can run a line forward to the dock from the bow cleat and back down against it using the "outside" engine. If the wind is blowing you onto the dock, compensate for the additional windage of the catamaran with extra stand-off space as you approach. Once alongside, secure the boat in the usual way with the bow, stern, and spring lines.

DEPARTING A SIDE TIE

Even with the wind pushing you onto the dock, with twin screws you can easily depart from a side tie in the way shown in the diagram at left. Double a spring line and lead it aft from the bow to leave stern first, or forward from the stern to leave bow first. Place a fender at the stern or the bow as needed. Rotate the boat by applying power against the spring with the outside engine. If the wind is light or in a favorable direction, you might not need to use the spring line.

DOCKING IN A SLIP

Entering a slip stern first gives the helmsman the better view and will allow the crew to step on and off at the low stern steps once the boat is secured.

Prepare the docklines ahead of time so the crew can drop loops over pilings and adjust the lines from on deck. Work with the wind, and focus on getting the windward lines attached first. Keep the lines away from the propellers.

Depending on the wind, adjacent boats, and the view from the helm, you may choose to motor past the slip in forward and then back in. Use the propellers to rotate the boat and to compensate for the effects of the wind.

Alternatively, back directly down the fairway and rotate into the slip using differential power on the twin screws.

Remember your pivot point, and apply reverse power — more to the outside engine than the inside engine — to make the turn. Maneuver the boat so you can attach the bow lines and springs to the appropriate pilings or cleats, then back in using bursts of power at idle in reverse.

DEPARTING A SLIP

Departing a slip when docked stern first is fairly straightforward. However, the number of steps involved means it takes practice, and the placement of pilings can make it difficult to double some of the lines prior to casting them off.

Prepare your docklines as best you can so you can easily slip them. Then remove any leeward lines you can reach.

Cast off the windward stern line and aft spring, taking care to keep the lines clear of the propellers. Ease forward, and use the forward spring as a breastline to hold

the boat against the wind until you can untie the leeward bow line and forward spring. Pivot the boat using differential power to bring the windward bow to where you can untie the windward bow line and forward spring.

(This maneuver is very nearly the reverse of the backing-in maneuver shown in the diagram below.)

Once the docklines are all clear, ease out into the fairway and rotate the boat in the desired direction.

....
TIP When planning any maneuver, watch for current and pay attention to the wind's strength and direction and the effect of the catamaran's high windage on its behavior.
....

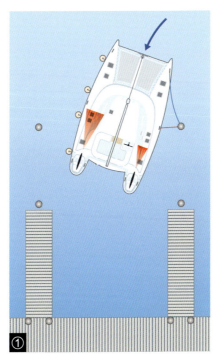

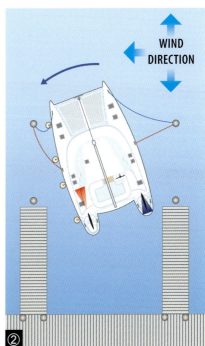

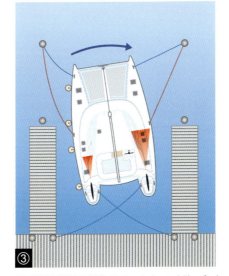

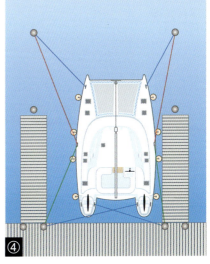

BACKING INTO A SLIP: Work with the wind. Place fenders as needed ahead of time. Start to windward of the slip and begin to rotate the boat using differential power. **1.** Place a bow line on the windward piling, plus a midships spring line to assist with the turn and hold the boat to the windward side of the slip. **2.** Continue to rotate the bow toward the leeward piling and attach the leeward bow line and spring line. **3.** Back in, using differential power to straighten up the boat, and attach the stern lines. **4.** Attach the aft spring lines and secure the boat so people can safely get off and on.

CHAPTER 5

Seamanship

Most of the skill set that falls under the broad heading of seamanship is applicable, and necessary, when operating a vessel of any kind, and cruising in a catamaran sailboat is in many ways little different from cruising in a monohull sailboat. The same fundamental knowledge about navigation, weather, sailing, and boat handling must be studied, acquired, and applied in the same way.

Specific types of craft, though, demand those skills in different degrees. We have already seen that the double-hull configuration affects the sailing and motoring characteristics of a catamaran. Together with other factors, such as positive flotation, these attributes influence how some onboard activities are carried out and also influence how emergencies can arise, play out, and are ultimately resolved.

DINGHY OPERATIONS

A virtual "dock" at the stern between a cruising catamaran's two hulls simplifies dinghy operations by providing an access point for safely boarding or disembarking from the dinghy. When it's not in use, and when the catamaran is under way, the dinghy can be stored out of harm's way in davits mounted on the aft crossbeam.

GREAT GAIN FOR LITTLE PAIN

Most catamarans are equipped with davits, a pair of small cranes used for hoisting the dinghy out of the water for storage. Although they create another set of tasks to perform when getting under way, davits are well worth the trouble, and are essential when dealing with a dinghy that will carry the larger crew a catamaran can accommodate.

HOISTING IN DAVITS

Lifting and storing a dinghy out of the water in davits lessens the risk of theft when the boat is at anchor and loss or damage that could be incurred when towing it. Suspended between the hulls, the dinghy takes up no deck space. Lifting points, and often a bridle, are fitted inside the dinghy, and a block and tackle system on the davits reduces the effort needed to raise it.

Make sure any charter briefing includes a demonstration of how to use the davits. Generally, the hoisting procedure is as follows:

① Close the dinghy's fuel tank vent.
② Remove loose gear from the dinghy.
③ Position the dinghy under the davits.
④ Lower the hoisting lines and attach the shackles to the lifting points or bridle.
⑤ If there is water in the dinghy, open the drain plug. If you expect rain, leave the plug out — just remember to replace it before launching.
⑥ Exit the dinghy.
⑦ Using the tackles, raise the bow and stern simultaneously.
⑧ When the dinghy is hard up against the davits, cleat off the hoisting tackles.
⑨ Secure the dinghy with bow and stern lines to prevent it from swinging. Check for chafe points and protect them if necessary.

For safety, do not operate the davits while anyone is in the dinghy.

This davit has a tackle that attaches to a bridle (blue webbing) fastened to the dinghy's floor.

The bridle suspends the dinghy so its weight is supported as evenly as possible between the two davits.

When the dinghy is fully hoisted in the davits, the crew can relax knowing it can't bump against the hull at night and it's unlikely to be stolen.

UNDER WAY

When under way, make sure the dinghy is fully hoisted in the davits and add supplemental lashings to prevent it from swinging from side to side, which is the major cause of chafe.

TOWING

For short inshore trips in calm seas you may choose to tow your dinghy instead of hoisting it. Depending on the speed at which you are towing, the best place for a dinghy might be on a bridle behind one hull. Sometimes, it might behave better on a bridle between both hulls so it's in front of the point where the wakes from the two hulls converge. Adjust the length of the bridle to suit the speed of the boat.

When slowing, haul in the towline so it doesn't get wrapped in a propeller. For backing, when anchoring or docking, tie the dinghy fore and aft on the outside of one of the hulls so it can't get between the hulls and under the bridgedeck.

ANCHORED OR MOORED

While maneuvering to set an anchor or pick up a mooring, haul in the towline and bring the dinghy alongside. When lying to a mooring or at anchor, you can let the dinghy trail astern in the wind, either on a single line or on a bridle between the two hulls. However, it's often better to tie it alongside a hull (with a fender for protection) to prevent it from getting between the hulls and under the bridgedeck. That also leaves the stern platforms clear for swimmers and those using water toys.

For security, and for peace of mind, hoist the dinghy in the davits overnight.

BOARDING AND EXITING

Boarding or disembarking from a dinghy is easy if you pull the dinghy between the catamaran's hulls and alongside a stern platform. You can then step or slide over the low side of the dinghy rather than the higher bow. Take the normal precautions: Step gently, never jump, and always maintain two or three points of contact.

When carrying the dinghy in the davits, use a bow line and a stern line to brace it against swinging, and use whatever means necessary to prevent the dinghy from chafing against the davits or the catamaran.

For boarding or disembarking, bring the dinghy alongside the transom platform and secure the painter. Passengers can then slide from a seated position on the stern to a seated position in the dinghy, and vice versa, without losing balance.

ANCHORING A CATAMARAN

The catamaran's maneuverability under power is a great help when anchoring, and the shoal draft can expand your choices in where you can anchor. Follow the same guidelines you would for any boat when selecting an anchorage but, when choosing the spot to anchor, allow for the tendency of a catamaran to "sail" toward and from its anchor.

GROUND TACKLE

Catamarans have significantly higher windage than monohulls of similar length, so they need proportionately larger anchors . . . and heavier anchor rodes to match. When selecting anchors and rodes, take into account the length of the boat, recommendations of the anchor manufacturers, and experience.

DECK ARRANGEMENT

The anchor windlass and chain locker are usually on the bridgedeck forward of the saloon, keeping the weight out of the bows. The anchor might be stowed in a roller on the forward crossbeam or below the forward part of the bridgedeck.

It's important on catamarans, once the anchor is set, to attach a bridle to the anchor rode. Its primary purpose is to keep the anchor rode centered between the bows and prevent the hulls from riding over the anchor chain. The bridle also acts as a snubber, taking the load off the windlass, and lessens the boat's tendency to "sail" around the anchor.

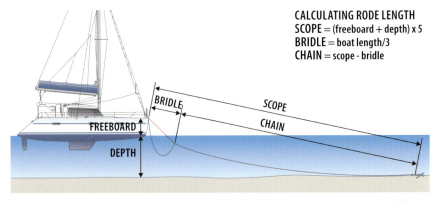

CALCULATING RODE LENGTH
SCOPE = (freeboard + depth) x 5
BRIDLE = boat length/3
CHAIN = scope - bridle

When calculating the length of anchor rode, include the effective length of the bridle. Example: For a boat length of 39 feet, freeboard 5 feet, water depth 10 feet: Bridle = 39/3 = 13 feet, Scope = (5 + 10) x 5 = 75 feet, Chain = 75 - 13 = 62 feet.

Your catamaran should be equipped with a rope bridle that has an end attached to each bow and a chain hook or shackle in the center for connecting it to the anchor chain. Each bridle arm should be equal in length to the beam of the boat so, when deployed, the angle between them is about 60 degrees. When not in use, the bridle is secured close to where the anchor is housed. Make sure the bridle is serviceable before you leave the dock.

CALCULATING SCOPE

Due to a catamaran's high windage, it's important to ensure that the anchor is set properly and with enough scope. Most charter catamarans are equipped with chain anchor rodes, so scope of 4:1 or 5:1 is sufficient when anchoring in protected harbors in normal weather conditions.

Remember to include in your scope calculation the freeboard at the bow as well as the depth. You can also include the bridle in your scope (for most bridles, 1/3 of the boat's length is about right).

ANCHORING STEP BY STEP

① Steering with the rudders and throttles, approach the spot where you plan to drop the anchor.
② Slow to a stop using gentle reverse power, then put the gearshifts in neutral.
③ Drop the anchor.
④ Pay out rode, laying it along the seabed as the boat drifts downwind. If there is no wind, back down slowly with the engines.
⑤ When you have payed out half the needed rode, secure it with the windlass and let the rode come taut to start setting the anchor.
⑥ Pay out more rode while drifting or powering slowly in astern.

This catamaran is anchored with the bridle doing the work and the anchor chain slack from the bridle to the windlass.

⑦ When the desired amount of rode is out, secure the windlass and gradually apply more load to the rode with the engines in astern. Use objects abeam as a range to ensure you're holding firm.

⑧ Attach the bridle.

ATTACHING THE BRIDLE

Don't be in too big a hurry to attach the bridle. You want to be absolutely sure the anchor is holding and will continue to hold. If the anchor should drag, your first response would normally be to pay out more rode to give the anchor another chance to set. You can't do that with the bridle attached — you have to haul back on the rode, disconnect the bridle, then pay out more rode.

Only when you are sure the anchor is firmly set, attach the bridle to the anchor chain with the shackle or chain hook. Let out more rode until the bridle is taking the load and the chain droops between the bridle and the roller. Apply reverse power once more to test the bridle.

MULTIPLE ANCHORS

For most conditions, a single anchor at the bow will suffice, but you might sometimes need a second anchor to limit how far the boat will swing if the wind or the current changes direction.

If you use a Bahamian moor, in which you deploy a second anchor from the bow at 180 degrees to the first, you must ensure the chain stays clear of the bows. The best way to do this, once you've set the second anchor, is to attach the second rode to the bridle. If you're chartering, ask your charter briefer to show you how to attach the second rode.

As the boat turns with the current, the two rodes might twist together, so keep an eye on them. If you remain anchored in the same place for a day or two, untwisting them could take a little time.

If you choose to set the second anchor from the stern, secure it to one of the stern cleats. A bridle should not be necessary, and it would interfere with dinghy operations and other activities.

On this boat, the anchors stow on the forward crossbeam and the windlass is on the bridgedeck forward of the mast. The bridle is attached to the anchor chain, (upper inset) after the rode has been payed out and the anchor is properly set. The anchor bridle is connected to the anchor chain with a shackle or a hook (lower inset).

On some boats, the anchor stows under the forward end of the bridgedeck with its bridle within easy reach.

MEDITERRANEAN MOOR

In some harbors and marinas in the Mediterranean and Caribbean, you'll be tying stern-to the seawall with your bow secured by an anchor or to a mooring. This "Mediterranean moor" is relatively easy to do in a catamaran as the twin screws allow you to hold position when needed and back down in any direction.

Before starting the maneuver, position fenders along both sides of the boat and at the stern, and have two stern lines attached and ready to go ashore.

If anchoring, drop the anchor a little to windward of your berth and far enough away from the seawall to allow sufficient scope for the depth and conditions. Back slowly toward the seawall while paying out anchor rode. Secure your stern lines ashore so they cross, then tension the anchor chain to hold your stern off the seawall. Do not rig the anchor bridle.

In many harbors, you will be attaching your bow to a mooring ball instead of an anchor. If so, prepare two long lines to make a bridle. In some marinas, an attendant in a dinghy might be on hand to help you attach your lines to the mooring buoy.

RAFTING AT ANCHOR

Rafting catamarans is potentially riskier than rafting monohulls, largely due to their greater windage. A three-catamaran raft is about the size of six monohulls of similar length.

While it's unlikely their masts will clash, catamarans do heave in swells and powerboat wakes, putting docklines under high stress. Many fenders must be used, and placed carefully where they do not contact hull windows.

Catamaran builders and charter companies discourage rafting.

MOORING BUOYS

Approaching a mooring under power with a catamaran is a little easier than with a monohull — if you've practiced station keeping using the twin screws. By adjusting the throttles, you can hold the boat head to wind or current and give the crew time to perform the foredeck work, which involves several steps.

PREPARATION

Normally, the best place to station the foredeck crew for picking up the mooring pendant with the boathook is on the trampoline next to one of the bows, near the root of the crossbeam. Which hull, port or starboard, depends on the helmsman's view, so you'd usually choose the same side as the helm. Use at least two crew if you have them, as the line handling takes several hands or great agility.

You'll use a bridle to keep the mooring ball centered between the hulls and also to hold the boat head to wind or current. Use two docklines for the bridle. Make fast one end of each arm of the bridle on the cleats on the port and starboard bows, then fake the lines down on the trampoline on the pick-up side (making sure they will lead clear of the headstay and any other rigging). Agree on the hand signals you'll use between helm and foredeck (see page 69).

> **TIP** *Commercial and official mooring buoys are generally quite secure, but beware of any unofficial or private ones. Take a swim (or the dinghy) and inspect any mooring that's the least suspect. Move if it looks unsafe.*

in some harbors, locals will offer to help you get attached to the mooring buoy. If you accept, make sure that you, as skipper of the catamaran, are in charge of the process.

APPROACH AND ATTACH

Motor slowly toward the buoy from directly downwind (or downcurrent) of it while steering with the propellers. Stop when the buoy is just inside the bow (you need good communication between foredeck and helm). Hold the boat in position while the crew picks up the pendant with the boathook, slips the working end of the nearside bridle line through the eye, and secures it to the bow cleat.

Keep the first bridle arm short at this time so the crew can still reach the pendant to run the second bridle arm through the eye and back to the opposite bow cleat. Once you have both arms secured to the pendant and to the boat, adjust the bridle so the pendant and buoy are centered between the hulls. For safety, always leave one bridle arm made fast while adjusting the other.

Throughout the process, the helmsman, guided by hand signals, must use the engines to hold the boat on station, applying power to give slack in the pendant when needed.

If you are picking up a buoy for a lunch stop in stable wind conditions, a single line threaded through the pendant eye and secured to each bow should suffice.

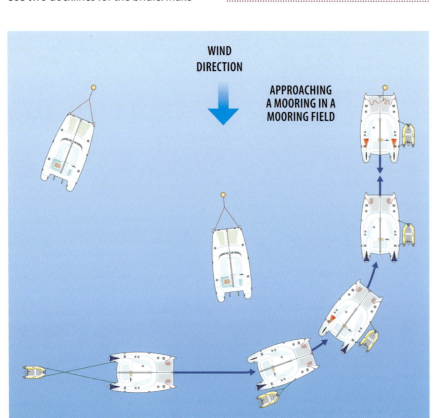

WIND DIRECTION

APPROACHING A MOORING IN A MOORING FIELD

If you're towing the dinghy, haul it up close and secure it alongside before you approach the mooring. Prepare the bridle well ahead of time. Bring the catamaran to a point downwind of the mooring, then ease toward it using power on each propeller as needed. Keep station while the crew retrieves the mooring pendant and attaches the two arms of the bridle.

The helmsman can lose sight of the mooring buoy behind the bow, so the foredeck crew must point toward it (1). It takes practice to stop the boat so the buoy is within the crew's reach (2). After threading the first arm of the bridle through the pendant (3), the crew still needs the helmsman to motor forward so he can reach the pendant to attach the second arm.

ALTERNATIVE TECHNIQUES

If the mooring does not have a pendant and you have to secure directly to the buoy, you might have to use the dinghy.

First, gain control of the mooring by dropping the bight of a line over the buoy to lasso it. Then, take one bridle arm at a time to the buoy in the dinghy — so you only have one line to control and keep away from the propeller.

DEPARTING A MOORING

When it's time to cast off the mooring, choose the direction in which you can depart that avoids obstructions or other boats. Release the bridle arm on that side first. This will swing the boat across the wind so it's pointing in your intended direction. Slip the second bridle line and you're off. Haul the lines aboard quickly to keep them out of the propellers.

The nearer boat has attached a bridle to the pendant on the mooring buoy. The other boat appears to have brought the pendant aboard and cleated it on deck, which is reasonable for a lunch stop on a quiet day but not for an overnight stay.

HAND SIGNALS

During anchoring and mooring maneuvers it's often hard for the helmsman to see what's happening in front of the boat. The distance between helm and foredeck hampers voice communications, so these maneuvers go more smoothly when the crew has agreed on hand signals to convey information and instructions.

Some catamaran crews include two-handed signals in their repertoires — one hand for each hull or engine. Here are some suggestions for both one- and two-handed signals that could be made by the foredeck crew when facing away from the helm.

Direction
Arm out straight in the direction of the object of interest

Stop both
Both fists clenched and held upward

Rotate to starboard
Hand above head moving in direction to rotate the boat when stationary

Forward both
Both arms, hands upward, rotating forward

Astern both
Both arms, palms downward, rotating backward

Bridle attached
Hands clasped above head

HANDLING EMERGENCIES

The majority of emergencies that might be encountered on a catamaran have similar causes as on a monohull and the actions required in response are mostly the same. However, some of those response techniques need to be adapted to accommodate differences in a catamaran's maneuverability and its general layout.

SAFETY EQUIPMENT

In the United States, federal requirements for carrying safety equipment are the same for a catamaran as for a monohull and are based on the boat's length (see page 77). However, for a vessel that has two hulls with an engine compartment in each of them, the requirements for fire extinguishers are inadequate. A prudent approach would be to treat the two hulls as separate boats by providing each hull with at least the minimum required

extinguishers, and adding a couple more in the cockpit and saloon to cover the bridgedeck area. A boat with a generator should have additional extinguishing capability for that compartment.

When chartering a catamaran, with the help of your briefer, make a complete inventory of its safety gear before you leave the dock. Draw up a station diagram showing where all safety-related items are located and post it where everyone on board can easily find it.

PERSONAL SAFETY

Don't be lured into a false sense of security by the catamaran's small heeling angles. In a seaway, unpredictable movements can catch you off balance. Try to maintain two or three points of contact when walking on deck or when climbing stairs and ladders.

Some catamarans have several deck levels, especially around the aft deck and cockpit. Watch where you place your feet but, at the same time, look for potential

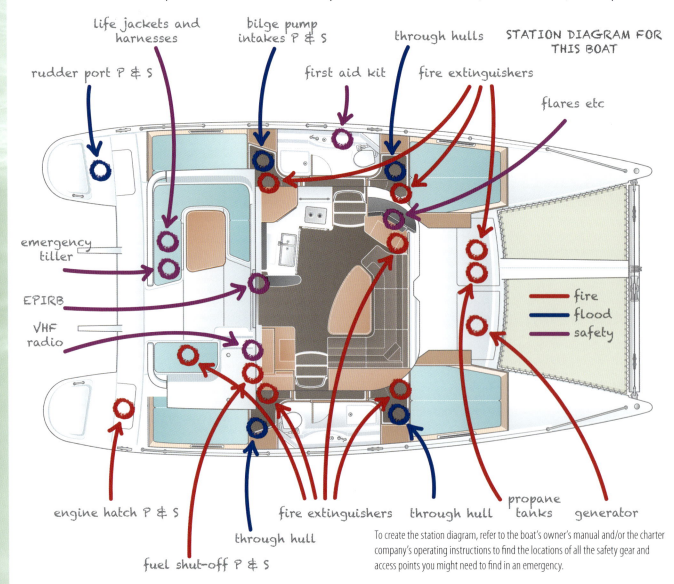

life jackets and harnesses

bilge pump intakes P & S

through hulls

STATION DIAGRAM FOR THIS BOAT

rudder port P & S

first aid kit

fire extinguishers

flares etc

emergency tiller

EPIRB

VHF radio

engine hatch P & S

fire extinguishers

through hull

propane tanks

generator

through hull

fuel shut-off P & S

— fire
— flood
— safety

To create the station diagram, refer to the boat's owner's manual and/or the charter company's operating instructions to find the locations of all the safety gear and access points you might need to find in an emergency.

head bangers, such as the cockpit roof. Avoid walking (or attempting to walk) on a trampoline when at sea, especially in big waves. The inertia of the flexible netting causes it to move in a different way from the boat — up when the boat goes down — and you have nothing but the netting itself to hold on to. If you must go forward when under way (to deal with a problem with the jib furler, for example), use the hulls, the catwalk, and the forward crossbeam — and clip on with your safety harness.

The guidelines for wearing PFDs and safety harnesses apply as on any boat.

JACKLINES

If you rig jacklines, their exact layout will depend on the boat's deck design. One method is to run them along the decks close to the deckhouse all the way to the bows, with another running across the bridgedeck forward of the deckhouse. This means unclipping and reclipping to get from the cockpit to the mast, but that's necessary if your tether is to be a safe length, i.e., 6 feet or shorter. If they are needed for access to the mast and the mainsail, run two additional jacklines diagonally across the deckhouse roof.

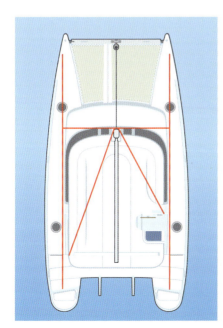

Jacklines should allow crew to get to as much of the deck as possible without having to unclip safety harnesses.

FIRE: REVIEW

Fire is potentially the most serious emergency that any boat could encounter. A fire that gets out of control will inevitably force you to abandon ship. Do your best to prevent fires by knowing their causes, and learn how to extinguish a fire in case one erupts.

FIRE PREVENTION

Electricity is the most common cause of fires on board. Most of the wiring is hidden, but where it's usually most vulnerable to damage is in the engine compartments — due to vibration — in an environment of potentially flammable oil and fuel. Regular inspections in all machinery spaces using sight, feel, and smell can reveal potential problem areas.

In the galley, adhere to the protocols for using propane (see page 38) and follow safe practices around open flames. Barbecue only at anchor or on a mooring when the wind is from ahead, and move the dinghy and water toys to the hull farthest from the grill and upwind of it.

FIRE RESPONSE

■ Shout "Fire, fire, fire!"
■ Get everyone on deck upwind of the fire and into PFDs.
■ Locate the fire and try to maneuver the boat so the wind can't spread the fire.
■ Fight the fire.
■ Assess the situation: If the fire threatens to get out of control, call Mayday and prepare to abandon ship.
■ Other actions you can take, if the circumstances permit, are to shut off the engines' fuel supplies and close the valves on the propane tanks.

FIRE-FIGHTING EQUIPMENT

Most marine extinguishers are of the B-C dry-powder variety that are effective on Class B fires (flammable liquids) and Class C fires (electrical fires). Armed with a bucket on a lanyard, you have access to unlimited water: Do not be afraid to use it on everything else (Class A fires).

A fire blanket, if the boat has one, is effective for smothering a galley fire.

FIGHTING THE FIRE

To use a fire extinguisher, think **PASS**:
■ **P**ull the pin.
■ **A**im at the base of the flames.
■ **S**queeze the trigger.
■ **S**weep from side to side.

Turn off the main DC and AC circuit breakers to avoid shocks and prevent an electrical fire from reigniting.

If smoke is coming out of the engine compartment, do not open the access hatch, as a rush of air could cause a smouldering fire to erupt in flames. If the compartment has an extinguishing system, activate it. If it doesn't, discharge an extinguisher into the fire port on the outside of the compartment.

For an electrical fire, use a fire extinguisher. If your extinguishers run out, keep fighting the fire with water, using buckets and any other means you have available. Drowned electronics are acceptable collateral damage if you manage to save the boat and crew.

Avoid being overcome by smoke and make sure you have an escape route — always keep yourself between the fire and your exit.

Make sure you know where all the fire extinguishers are located and memorize the operating instructions.

MAN OVERBOARD

The sailing and handling characteristics of a catamaran affect the way you maneuver to recover a man overboard (MOB), whether under sail, under power, or using a combination of both.

A catamaran's low stern platforms, and sometimes the davits, offer options for recovering an MOB.

CATAMARAN FACTORS

When adapting traditional MOB recovery methods, you must take into account the catamaran's performance characteristics.

■ A catamaran is faster on some points of sail than a monohull and might travel farther away from the MOB during the initial reaction period.

■ A catamaran does not turn as sharply, and is markedly slower and more difficult to tack. If the maneuver that offers the most direct return involves tacking, you may need assistance from the engines.

■ When approaching an MOB at a slow speed, compensate for the catamaran's pronounced leeway. Avoid letting the boat get too far downwind of the MOB.

■ Visibility from the helm station is often limited, especially if the MOB recovery is on the opposite side of the boat from the helm. If feasible, maneuver to pick up the MOB on the same side as the helm.

■ High freeboard makes recovery over the side difficult. The low sterns offer easier and more sheltered access.

■ Due to the catamaran's narrow hulls, an MOB alongside a hull will be very close to a propeller.

MOB UNDER SAIL

The initial actions — Yell, Throw, Point, Set, Call — are the same as for any MOB incident. The recovery course you choose will depend on the sailing characteristics of the particular boat, the crew's skill, and possibly the point of sail you were on when the MOB occurred. The goal is to bring the boat to the MOB as quickly as possible. Be flexible. Practice so you can acquire the skills that will enable you to improvise and make the right choices. Here are some of your options:

■ From a broad reach or downwind course, head up toward a beam reach, tack as soon as you are able, and return on a close reach. Control speed by easing or trimming the sheets and bring the boat to a stop to windward of the MOB.

■ From a beam reach, sail five to ten boat lengths, tack, and sail back to a point from which you can turn to make your final approach on a close reach as above. Allow for leeway. You don't want to get too far downwind of the MOB before setting up for your final approach.

■ From a close-hauled or close-reaching course, tack and leave the jib backed. The boat will stop hove-to and drift slowly downwind. Use the engines to maneuver forward or backward as necessary to reach the MOB.

MOB USING SAIL AND POWER

The maneuvers described above are difficult to accomplish under sail alone, especially in less than ideal conditions. For any MOB maneuver, if using the engines is likely to result in a more timely pickup, use them, but with caution.

Before turning on an engine, make sure no lines are in the water to foul a propeller. When throwing a rescue line to an MOB, keep it away from the propellers — shut down an engine if necessary.

If your sailing maneuver requires you to tack, use the outside engine to help with the turn so you don't get stuck in irons and can quickly return to the MOB. By using power, you can completely luff

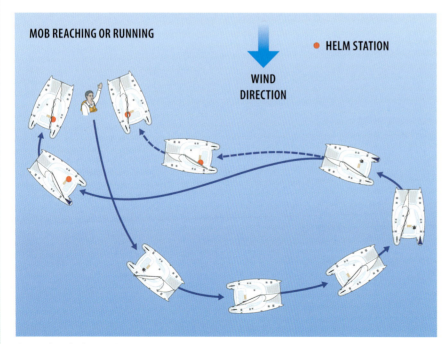

MOB REACHING OR RUNNING

● HELM STATION

WIND DIRECTION

The Broad-Reach Close-Reach return maneuver works quite well with a catamaran, but allow for the catamaran's leeway. Return to the MOB by sailing more on a beam reach than a close reach. Try to put the MOB on the same side as the helm station (note the alternatives shown). Time is of the essence: Don't hesitate to use the engines to help you through the tack.

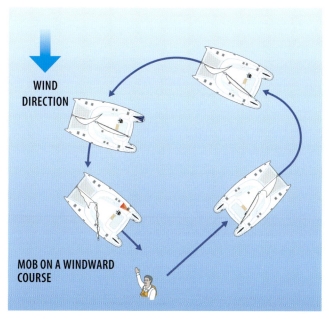

WIND DIRECTION

MOB ON A WINDWARD COURSE

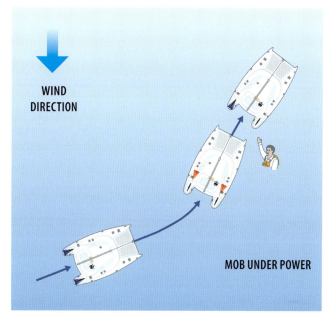

WIND DIRECTION

MOB UNDER POWER

From a windward course, heave-to to stop the boat, then use the engines to maneuver toward the MOB. Shut down the engine nearer the MOB. Furl the jib when you can.

When retrieving an MOB under power, throw a line to him from forward. Use the engine on the opposite side (if needed) to bring him to the stern, then shut down the nearer one.

or even drop or furl the sails and focus more on getting into the correct position to pick up the MOB. You can use one engine to help hold the boat in place, but make absolutely sure to **shut down** the engine on the MOB side so a spinning propeller does not become an issue.

MOB UNDER POWER

If a person falls overboard while the catamaran is under power, immediately shift both engines into neutral. Once the MOB is well clear of the propellers, use both engines to return to the MOB.

Maneuver the boat to windward of the MOB so someone standing forward of the beam can throw him a line. Once the MOB has hold of the line, **shut down** the engine on that side.

MOB RECOVERY

Whether under sail or power, get a line to the MOB as soon as possible, and offer some flotation if he is not wearing a PFD. The high freeboard will make lifting the MOB up and over the side extremely difficult. If the sea state allows, guide the MOB to the stern where you can assist him onto a transom or hoist him to the deck between the hulls (whichever is

more sheltered and accessible) with the help of a davit or halyard.

Because of the proximity of the propellers, make sure the engines are shut down when an MOB is anywhere near the stern. If you need to use an engine to hold the boat in position, use the one on the opposite side from the recovery area.

ANCILLARY EQUIPMENT

It's worth doing anything you can to make an MOB incident end with a swift

and effective recovery. This includes having specialized equipment on board.

Several useful devices are available, including recovery lines made of floating line and prepacked in bags that make them easy to throw toward an MOB.

Another recovery aid found on many boats is the LifeSling, a flotation collar attached to a length of floating line. The collar is intended to be dropped into the water and the line, which is tied to the boat, payed out. The goal then is to drag the line to where the MOB can grab it.

The LifeSling is a self-contained MOB recovery device. As demonstrated at the US Naval Academy, a lone crew can deploy it, drag the flotation collar to the MOB, and, using a halyard attached to the integral harness, haul the MOB aboard.

ENGINE FAILURE

An engine failure on a sailboat is often more an inconvenience than an emergency but, on occasion, you might need to take action to prevent a situation from becoming an emergency.

ONE ENGINE

Since motoring or motorsailing with one engine is a normal fuel-saving strategy, losing one engine is not by itself an emergency. You will be able to motor to a safe haven on the remaining engine, but docking the boat will be difficult because you will have lost much of your ability to steer at low speeds. This is where a little time spent practicing single-engine maneuvers will pay dividends.

Getting alongside a dock will be easier than entering a slip. Use all your fenders and plan how you can best use spring lines and the remaining engine to bring the boat into the dock. Look for a berth where the wind will be your ally.

On a charter, call the charter base, as the staff will want to figure out the cause of the failure and get you going again.

SEEK THE CAUSE

If an engine stops, try to find out why, in case you risk losing both.

If you hear an alarm, look at the warning lights to see if the alarm is for low oil pressure or engine temperature. If the latter, look for water exiting with the exhaust. If there is none, shut down the engine and check the raw-water intake strainer for a blockage.

If the oil-pressure alarm sounded, shut down the engine, wait a few minutes, and check the oil level.

Neither of these issues should affect the second engine, but if an engine stopped and you heard no alarm, the problem could be with the fuel supply. This might indicate a potential problem for the second engine, especially if they share a fuel tank. Check the fuel supply, filters, and vent lines.

A line around a propeller could also stop an engine.

NO ENGINES

If you lose both engines, you will have to think fast. Your first priority is the safety of the crew and boat. Raise sail so you can steer the boat to a safe area. If you are becalmed, make a Securité call on VHF 16 to alert nearby boats that you are limited in your ability to maneuver.

If you are unable to sail due to lack of wind or for any other reason, anchor the boat if that's necessary to prevent it from drifting into danger. Call for assistance if you need it — sooner rather than later.

TAKING ON WATER

Flooding will probably render a catamaran unmaneuverable, but since a catamaran should remain afloat, taking on water is not as desperate a situation as it might be on a monohull.

TAKE "FLOOD STATIONS"

At the first indication that the boat is taking on water, ensure that the electric bilge pumps are switched on and instruct crew to work the manual bilge pump in the affected hull(s). Then look for where the water is coming from.

Taste the water. Unless you are on a lake, fresh water means the problem is with your freshwater system. Salt water can only come from outside the boat.

Check the escape hatches and all the through-hull fittings. Also check the saildrive seals or the stern glands. If the boat suffered an impact, look for structural damage. Stem the water ingress as best you can by bracing padding or blankets against any hole.

If your catamaran has watertight compartments in the bow and/or stern and the water ingress is in one of them, make sure that compartment's drain valve remains closed. It will only fill so far, and pumping will be futile until the leak is stopped.

Call for assistance if flooding is severe or you are unable to stop the leak. It's better to call early than too late.

Flooding should not force you to abandon ship. Because of the way they are built, most catamarans will stay afloat, especially if the flooding is limited to one hull. A large catamaran is far more visible to rescuers than a tiny life raft and, with its stores and water, is a far better place to await rescue.

A saildrive passes through a large hole in the hull. If the seal is damaged, the compartment will quickly flood. The engine's raw-water intake (valve with red handle) is on the drive unit.

RUNNING AGROUND

A catamaran's shallow draft allows you to stray a little farther from deep water without risking running aground. However, if you stray too far, you'll find it is a lot more difficult to refloat a grounded catamaran than it is a grounded monohull.

When a daggerboard is down, a catamaran is no longer a shoal-draft sailboat, so watch the depth carefully.

GETTING OFF

A grounded monohull can be heeled to reduce its draft, but that does not work so well with a catamaran, especially if both hulls are aground. If you run aground while sailing to windward, easing the sheets so the sails luff might lift the leeward hull the few inches needed.

In many instances of grounding, the shallow keels of a cruising catamaran will protect the props and rudders, allowing you to use the engines to maneuver the boat off the ground. After furling the sails, and once you've determined where deeper water lies, you might be able to back the boat off using the engines.

If powering off fails, consider kedging or taking a tow. Until the keels are free, tow or kedge either straight forward or straight aft to avoid applying excessive torque to the catamaran's structure.

DAGGERBOARDS AND GROUNDING

A daggerboard is likely to break in a hard or high-speed grounding. While that probably means the boat is no longer aground, the impact could damage the daggerboard trunk, which might result in a leak.

If a daggerboard does strike bottom, stop the boat from sailing, raise the other board if it's down (to avoid damaging it too), and check for water ingress through or around the trunk. Try to raise the damaged daggerboard. You might have to attach a halyard to it to give you the necessary purchase.

With no keels to protect them, the rudders and props will be damaged if a daggerboard boat runs aground with the boards raised.

STEERING FAILURE

If you lose steering in a catamaran, the problem will be either a failure in the steering linkage, the loss of a rudder, or a rudder jam as a result of a grounding or collision with a floating object.

With the deckhouse in the way, the view from the emergency tiller is limited, so post lookouts.

RESPONSE AND REMEDIES

If the manual steering becomes stiff, first check that the autopilot has not been accidentally activated. This does happen if someone bumps the "Auto" button! Next, inspect the steering linkage and the rudder stocks to see if any gear stowed nearby has become loose and caused an obstruction.

If the steering wheel turns freely but there is no steering response, the fault is very likely in the linkage. To regain steering, activate the autopilot or use the emergency tiller. Steering with an emergency tiller is no easy feat, as the force on the rudders can be strong. The deckhouse will limit the view forward, so post lookouts.

You might be able to repair a loose or

disconnected cable, but to do so safely you will need to immobilize the rudders somehow. If the linkage is working but you have little steering response, you may have lost one of the rudders.

If you are unable to turn the wheel because a rudder is jammed, neither the autopilot nor the emergency tiller will help. You'll need the assistance of a towboat to get safely into port.

A lost or jammed rudder resulting from an impact with a floating object or a hard grounding could be accompanied by serious ingress of water where the rudder stock enters the hull. The likelihood of losing both rudders is minimal unless you've run hard aground.

In any event, steer the boat to safety as best you can by trimming the sails and

using differential power settings on the engines. Be prepared to drop the anchor if you are in danger of running aground. Make a Securité call on VHF 16 to alert other vessels in the area that you are "Not Under Command." Call for assistance.

CAPSIZE

Catamaran capsizes are rare. When they do occur, they are usually due to two causes: being in the wrong place at the wrong time or operator error. Most cruising sailors can avoid the first cause by carefully choosing where and when to go sailing and by paying close attention to the weather.

CAPSIZE PREVENTION

You can reduce the risk of operator error by reading the sailing instructions for the boat and by learning to read the signs of the boat being overpowered. Sail within your own limits and those of your crew as well as within the limits of the boat.

Catamarans feel stable even in strong winds because they heel so little. The biggest dangers are being overpowered by too much sail or traveling too fast down a wave and having one or both bows dig in and the boat pitchpole.

To prevent capsize, always reef within the recommended wind speeds, and remember that sea state must be a contributing factor in your decisions. When stowing provisions and gear, distribute the weight evenly and be careful not to overload the bows.

POST-CAPSIZE PROCEDURES

In the very unlikely event of capsize, a cruising catamaran will remain inverted but afloat. For that reason, and because it's a large visible target for search and rescue responders, always stay with the boat while it's afloat.

Safety regulations require cruising catamarans to have escape hatches built into them. They are usually in the inboard sides of the hulls or the underside of the bridgedeck. it's essential to know where they are and how they open, but they must be kept shut when under way. If you are inside when the boat is inverted, they are your primary means of escape. If you are outside the boat, they could possibly give you access to the inside for shelter and to stores of food and water.

The first priority after a capsize is to look to the safety of your crew:

- Make a head count as soon as you can and check everyone for injuries.
- Secure the crew to the inverted boat — many catamarans have pad eyes and jacklines attached to the underside for this purpose.
- Secure the ditch bag and life raft and salvage whatever you can from the boat to assist your rescue and provide comfort and sustenance for your crew.
- Send distress signals by whatever means available — EPIRB, VHF radio and, if other vessels are in sight, flares.

ABANDON SHIP

Since a catamaran will normally float after a capsize or when flooded, fire is the only event that should force you to abandon it. Even so, a capsize or serious flooding will deprive you of shelter, most of your communications, and food and water, leaving you with whatever is stored in your life raft and ditch bag. You will be essentially "abandoning in place."

If you don't have a ditch bag (see below), you will need to gather together as much of your survival equipment as you can: flares, EPIRB, radio, satellite phone, survival rations, and drinking water. If you have time, also try to collect passports, cash, credit cards, the ship's papers, and prescription medications.

DITCH BAG

A ditch bag is not usually considered necessary when sailing on inland or coastal waters, even though accidents can happen anywhere. The purpose of the ditch bag is to provide you with the means to call for help and to survive while waiting for help to arrive.

Among the items normally stored in a ditch bag, which should be waterproof, buoyant, and highly visible, are a PLB, a handheld VHF radio, a visual signaling device, a knife, a flashlight, water, and food. Passports and other personal items can be stored in a separate bag.

Stow the ditch bag where you'll have the best chance of retrieving it when needed. That might be in a locker close to where the life raft is stored.

While a cruising catamaran capsize is a rarity, some countries require manufacturers to equip cats with escape hatches in the hulls. It's tempting to open them when at anchor for ventilation, but they must always be closed and locked before getting under way. On some catamarans, the hatches are sealed and must be broken with a hammer if needed.

SAFETY EQUIPMENT: REVIEW

US law requires that vessels operating in US waters, and US documented vessels operating anywhere, carry certain safety equipment and other materials. The requirements that apply to sailboats and powerboats from 26 to 65 feet are listed in the table. A charter boat operating in US waters must have this equipment on board. Outside the US, charter boats must be equipped to comply with local laws and regulations.

ADDITIONAL EQUIPMENT

ASA recommends that, in addition to the required safety equipment, the items listed below should be part of a sailboat's standard outfit.

- Anchors (at least two) with rodes
- Binoculars
- Boathook
- Bucket (and lanyard)
- Charts and cruising guides
- Cleaning materials for the deck
- Deck-plate key
- Docklines (at least six)
- Fenders (at least four)
- First-aid kit
- Flashlights
- Hand-bearing compass
- Knife
- Manuals for onboard equipment
- Plotting tools: parallel rule, dividers, pencils
- Radar reflector
- Safety harnesses
- Safety tethers
- Spare lines (large and small)
- Swim/boarding ladder
- Tide tables
- Timepiece
- Toolkit
- VHF Radio
- Water hose with spray nozzle

US FEDERAL CARRIAGE REQUIREMENTS BY BOAT SIZE:

		26 - 40 ft	40 - 65 ft
REGISTRATION AND NUMBERS		Hull numbers + certificate + documentation number (if documented)	Hull numbers + certificate + documentation number (if documented)
PERSONAL FLOTATION DEVICES		One approved PFD for each person on board plus one throwable PFD	One approved PFD for each person on board plus one throwable PFD
VISUAL DISTRESS SIGNALS	day	Distress flag and/or 3 smoke or day/ night flares	Distress flag and/or 3 smoke or day/ night flares
	night	3 night flares	3 night flares
FIRE EXTINGUISHERS		2 B-I or 1 B-II	3 B-I or 1 B-I + 1 B-II
SOUND-PRODUCING DEVICE		Hand-held or mouth-blown horn	Whistle per Navigation Rules
NAVIGATION LIGHTS	optional for under sail only	Sidelights + stern light in tricolor + masthead lantern	Sidelights + stern light in tricolor + masthead lantern
	required	sidelights + sternlight + masthead light	sidelights + sternlight + masthead light
PLACARDS		Discharge of oil + MARPOL discharge of garbage	Discharge of oil + MARPOL discharge of garbage + Waste management
MARINE SANITATION DEVICE		Type I, Type II, or Type III	Type I, Type II, or Type III
NAVIGATION RULES		Not required	Required

PURSUE THE DREAM

The sport of sailing can provide you with a lifetime of enjoyment. And, as you've learned from this book, sailing and cruising on a catamaran can be especially rewarding.

If you are one of the many who have been reading this book in conjunction with training for the ASA114 Cruising Catamaran Standard, you will be certified to this ASA standard. As any sailor knows, learning the ropes is just the first step.

You now have the knowledge and the tools, and it is up to you to begin to use

them in real-life situations, building your experience with time on the water. For it is through practice — hours of sailing on different boats, in different roles, and in different places — that you will become a true sailor. But make no mistake, in sailing there's always more to learn — and that's a large part of the sport's allure.

When you are ready, you can continue your formal training through ASA's advanced-level certifications, such as Advanced Coastal Cruising, Celestial Navigation, or the coveted Offshore Passagemaking Standard. Until then, get out there and have some fun.

If you are like me, you'll be doing it on a boat with two hulls!

Cam Lewis

REVIEW QUESTIONS (see page 90 for answers)

FILL IN THE BLANK

1 The catamaran's fully-battened mainsail is very heavy; hoisting is made easier by using a halyard with a ___2:1___ ___purchase___.

2 When sailing to windward, the high profile of a catamaran creates ___windage___ that slows boat speed. Combined with its increased ___leeway___ due to the shoal-draft keels, this requires a catamaran to sail at ___wider___ angles and ___faster___ boat speeds than a monohull to achieve good windward VMG.

3 When trimming the mainsail for best close-hauled performance, it is best to center the boom with the ___traveler___ and then use the ___mainsheet___ to trim the sail for optimum twist.

4 Due to its large mainsail, the catamaran is susceptible to weather-vaning if boat speed is too low when ___tacking___. If the boat stalls, the jib may be ___backed___ to assist the turn.

5 The key to effective tacking is to have best possible boat speed, be close-hauled, turn the wheel ___steadily___, ease the traveler a little and quickly trim the ___jib___ on the new side. Building ___speed___ is important before trimming the ___mainsail___ onto the new close-hauled course.

6 The catamaran's faster ___boat___ ___speed___ exaggerates the ___apparent___ wind speed and angle, which affect how a catamaran sailor should steer and trim.

7 When sailing to windward, daggerboards should be ___lowered___ to reduce leeway. When sailing downwind, daggerboards should be ___retracted___ to reduce drag and turbulence.

8 When sailing downwind, find your course for best downwind VMG by sailing a ___slalom___ course and noting boat speed and apparent wind speed on different headings.

9 When jibing a catamaran, it's important to jibe ___slowly___ and use the traveler and mainsheet to control the large ___mainsail___.

10 A lack of heeling and reduced weather helm reduce the sensory cues that indicate when to reef. Consult the manufacturer's charts that recommend the ___wind___ ___speeds___ at which to reef. ___Sea___ state and approaching squalls should also be factored into the skipper's decision.

11 To maintain better control when sailing in gusty conditions, ___head___ ___up___ in gusts when sailing to windward, and ___bear___ ___away___ when sailing downwind.

12 The large size of the catamaran, which can cause difficulties when docking or maneuvering under power, is greatly overcome by the use of its ___twin___ screws .

13 Slow-speed maneuvering is enhanced by using ___different___ power and direction of thrust, which moves the pivot point toward the ___hull___ with the least thrust.

14 Care must be taken when slow-speed maneuvering under power in windy conditions due to the shoal ___Keels___ and the ___windge___ of the high freeboard and large deckhouse.

15 Motorsailing with one engine saves ___fuel___ but affects the balance of the boat.

16 Rudders become ineffective at low speeds. Therefore, when docking a catamaran, center the ___wheel___ and maneuver the boat with the two ___engines___.

17 Name four of the steps involved to safely hoist and secure a dinghy in davits: ___close tank vent___, ___remove gear low d___, _____, _____.

18 Dinghy boarding is conveniently done at the ___transom___, which offers a low step to embark. Remember to maintain three ___point___ ___of___ ___contact___ at all times.

19 When picking up a mooring buoy, prepare the ___bridle___ lines in advance and approach directly ___upwind___ or into the current, aiming to pick up the mooring buoy just inside the bow.

20 Anchoring or picking up a mooring buoy goes far more smoothly if the person at the bow uses a set of agreed ___hand___ ___signals___ to communicate with the helm.

21 The purpose of the ___bridle___ is to keep an anchor or mooring ball centered between the two hulls.

22 Name four features of catamaran structure and performance that affect Man Overboard recovery. _____, _____, _____, _____.

23 The key to avoiding a Man Overboard situation is to keep the crew safely on board by rigging ___jacklines___ and using ___tethers___.

24 One of the primary causes of catamaran capsize is being ___overpowered___ because of having too much sail set.

25 List five post-capsize response procedures. _____, _____, _____, _____, _____.

GLOSSARY

A

Aback Of a sail, when the wind is on the "wrong" side

Abeam Off the boat at right angles to its centerline

Accommodations The living quarters inside a boat

Aft Toward the *stern* or behind the boat

Aground When the *hull* or *keel* is touching the *bottom*

Aloft Above the *deck*, usually in the *rig*

Amidships At or toward the middle of the boat

Amp-hour A measure of electricity consumption and battery capacity: one amp of current for one hour

Anchor A device lowered to the *bottom* while *secured* to the boat to hold the boat stationary

Angle of attack The angle between the apparent wind and the chord of a sail

Apparent wind The combination of *true wind* and the wind effect of motion as felt aboard a moving boat

Astern Behind the *stern*

Athwartships Across the boat from side to side

Autopilot A device that steers a boat automatically

B

Backing The act of setting a sail *aback*

Backstay A wire support from the top of the *mast* to the *stern*

Backwinding Similar to *backing*

Ballast Weight placed low in the boat to give it stability

Batten A slat inserted in the *leech* of a sail to support the *sailcloth*

Batten pocket A pocket sewn into the sail to hold a *batten*

Beam The width of a boat at its widest point

Beam reach The *point of sail* where the wind is *abeam* of the boat

Bear away To turn the boat away from the wind, *fall off*

Bearing The direction in degrees toward one object from another

Beat, beating To sail to *windward* *close-hauled*

Berth (1) A bed on a boat

Berth (2) Where a boat ties up or *docks*

Bilge The lowest interior regions of the *hull*

Bilge pump A pump for removing water from the bilge

Block A pulley

Boathook A pole with a hook on one end useful for snagging a *line* or a ring

Boom The *spar* that supports the *foot* of the *mainsail*

Boom vang An item of *running rigging* used to hold down the *boom*

Bottom The seabed or bed under any body of water

Bow The *forward* part of a boat

Bowline A *knot* that forms a loop in the end of a *line*

Bow line A *dockline* tied between the *bow* of a boat and a *dock*

Bridgedeck The deck structure spanning the *hulls* of a *catamaran*

Bridgedeck clearance The distance from the water's surface to the underside of the *bridgedeck*

Bridle (1) A line fixed at both ends that spreads the force on another line, a towline, e.g., attached at its midpoint

Bridle (2) A pair of lines used to spread the load from a central connecting point to two separate points (used when anchored or moored)

Broad reach The *point of sail* between a *beam reach* and a *run*

Bulkhead An upright partition in the interior of a boat

By the lee Sailing on a *run* with the wind on the same side as the *mainsail*

C

Cabin A room in the interior of a boat

Capsize To turn over

Cast off To undo completely a *line* that has been *secured*

Catamaran A boat with two *hulls*

Catwalk A solid walkway along the centerline between the bridgedeck and the forward *crossbeam* (also ramp)

Centerboard A board that pivots down from the bottom of the boat to provide sideways resistance

Chafe Damage caused to a sail or a *line* by rubbing

Chainplate Metal fabrication attached to the *hull* and to which a *stay* or *shroud* is connected

Chart table A table or desk used when navigating

Chock A fixed *fairlead* through which *dock lines* are led

Cleat A fitting used to *secure* a *line*

Clew The *aft* lower corner of a sail

Close-hauled The *point of sail* where a boat sails as close to the wind as possible

Close reach The *point of sail* between *close-hauled* and a *beam reach*

Cockpit The area of the boat, usually recessed into the *deck*, from which the boat is steered and sailed

Course The direction of intended travel chosen when navigating

Cringle An eye formed by sewing a rope or metal ring into, e.g., a sail

Crossbeam A beam that connects the *hulls* of a *catamaran*

D

Daggerboard A board that slides vertically through a trunk in the *hull* to provide lateral resistance

Davit A small crane mounted on deck (usually as a pair) used to hoist and *secure* a *dinghy* out of the water

Deck The generally horizontal surface that encloses the top of the *hull*

Deckhouse The *cabin* on top of a *bridgedeck* on a *catamaran*

Depth The curvature of a sail from *luff* to *leech*

Diamond stays Wires supported by struts in a diamond shape to keep a *mast* in column

Dinghy A small boat

Dock (1) A place where a vessel is *berthed*, but generally used to refer to the pier, quay, or pontoon to which it's tied when in that *berth*

Dock (2) To bring a boat to its *dock*

Dockline A *line* used to tie a boat in its *dock*

Docking The process of bringing a boat into its *dock*

Dolphin striker A braced strut beneath a *crossbeam* that supports the *mast*

Downwind In the direction toward which the wind is blowing

Draft (1) The depth of a boat below the water

Draft (2) The curvature of a sail

Draft position The fore-and-aft position where a sail's *depth* is greatest

Drag Of an *anchor*, to slide along the seabed, not hold

Drive train The engine, *propeller*, and the associated components that "drive" a boat mechanically

E

Ease To let out a *line* that has load on it

Escape hatch A *hatch* in a catamaran that allows egress after a *capsize*

F

Fair Smooth, unobstructed

Fairlead A *fitting* used to lead a *line fair* and at the correct angle to a *winch*, *cleat*, or other *fitting*.

Fake, flake To lay out a *line* in parallel lengths so it can run freely

Fall off To turn away from the wind, *bear away*

Fender A cushion, usually an inflated cylinder of rubber or similar material, placed between a boat and a *dock*

Fitting A piece of hardware that is fixed to the boat or its *spars*

Flake To lay in even loose folds, as a sail

Flybridge A helm station located on top of the *deckhouse*

Foot The bottom edge of a sail

Foot off *Bear away* from *close-hauled* to gain speed

Fore-and-aft The direction parallel with the centerline of a boat

Foredeck The *forward* part of the *deck*, usually forward of the forwardmost *mast*

Fore-reach Heavy-weather tactic of sailing slowly to *windward* under much-reduced canvas

Foresail A sail set *forward* of the *mainsail*, often a *jib* or a *headsail*

Forestay A *stay* that supports the *mast* from *forward*

Forward Toward the *bow*

Fouled Tangled, snagged

Fractional rig A *rig* configuration in which the *forestay* is attached at some distance below the *masthead*

Freeboard The height of the *hull* above the *waterline*

Full About a sail, when it is not flapping or *luffing*

Furl To stow a sail on a *spar* or a *stay*

G

Galley A kitchen on a boat

Going astern To be moving backward

Gooseneck An articulated fitting that connects a *boom* to a *mast*

Grommet A metal ring set into a sail

Ground tackle Collective term for a boat's *anchors* and their *rodes*

Gust A brief increase in wind speed

H

Halyard A *line* used to raise and lower a sail

Hatch A covered opening in the *deck*

Head (1) The top of a sail

Head (2) Toilet compartment on a boat

Head to wind A boat's position when its *bow* is pointing directly into the wind

Headboard A reinforcement at the *head* of a sail

Head down To steer away from the wind, *bear away*, *fall off*

Header A wind shift in which the wind shifts forward

Headsail Any sail set *forward* of the forwardmost *mast*; a *jib*

Headstay The *stay* between the top of the *mast* and the *bow*

Head up To steer more toward the wind

Headway Motion in a forward direction

Heave-to To hold a boat almost stationary by setting the sails and *rudder* in opposition

Heel (Of a boat) to lean sideways under the pressure of the wind on the sails

Helm The *tiller* or wheel with which the boat is steered

Helmsman The person at the *helm* steering the boat

Helm station The steering position

Hoist To haul *aloft*

Holding tank A tank in which sewage is stored

Hull The watertight structural shell of a boat.

I

Inboard Toward the centerline of the boat; inside the *hull*

In irons Of a boat that's *head to wind*, having lost all *headway*

Inverter An electrical device that converts direct current to alternating current

J

Jackline A *line* secured to the deck as a place to attach *safety tethers*

Jib A triangular sail set *forward* of the *mainmast*

Jibe To turn the boat so that its *stern* passes through the wind

Jibsheet A *line* attached to the *clew* of a *jib* used to adjust its angle to the wind

K

Kedge A supplementary *anchor*

Kedge off Use an *anchor* to haul a grounded boat off the *bottom*

Keel The main structural member along the bottom of a boat's *hull*; on a sailboat often an appended fin-shaped structure that contains *ballast*

Keelboat A sailboat that has a *keel* and *ballast*, usually combined

Knot (1) A fastening made by entwining a rope, *line*, or cord with itself or with other ropes, lines, or cords

Knot (2) Unit of speed: one nautical mile (6,076 feet) per hour

L

Lazy Of, for example, a *jibsheet*, the windward one that's not under load

Lazy-jacks A system of lines run from *mast* to *boom* to hold a dropped sail above the *boom*

Leech The *after* edge of a sail

Lee Sheltered area to *leeward* of something (boat, building, island) that's protected from the wind

Lee helm The tendency of a sailboat when sailing to turn *downwind*

Lee side The side away from the wind, or *downwind* side

Lee shore A shore toward which the wind is blowing

Leeward The direction, or side of the boat, away from the wind

Lifeline A wire supported on *stanchions* around the perimeter of the *deck* to prevent crew from falling overboard

Lift A wind shift in which the wind shifts aft

Line A length of *rope* that has a specific purpose on board

Locker A storage compartment

Luff (1) The *forward* edge of a sail

Luff (2) The fluttering of a sail when the angle of attack is too small

Luff (3) To *head up* so that the sails *luff*

M

Mainsail The sail attached to the *aft* side of the mainmast

Mainsheet The line used to control the main *boom* and thus also to *trim* the *mainsail*

Make fast To *secure*, as when tying a *line* to a *cleat*

Mast A fixed vertical *spar* that holds up a sail or sails

Masthead The top of a *mast*

Masthead fly A wind vane fitted at the *masthead*

Masthead rig A sailboat *rig* where the *headstay* is attached at the *masthead*

Mediterranean moor To *moor* a boat by means of an *anchor* in the harbor and the *stern* tied to a *quay* or *pier*

Moor To tie up (a boat)

Mooring A permanently set *anchor*

Mooring buoy A *buoy* attached to a *mooring* and to which a boat can be *moored*

Motorsailing Motoring while also using the sails for propulsion

Multihull A boat with more than one *hull*

N

Nacelle A forward projection of a *bridgedeck*

No-discharge zone An area where sewage, treated or untreated, may not be discharged into the water

No-sail zone The zone in relation to the wind where the sails cannot generate power

O

Off the wind Any *point of sail* where the wind is *abaft* the *beam*

On the wind Any *point of sail* where the wind is *forward* of the *beam*

Outboard (1) Away from the centerline of a boat; outside the *gunwale*

Outboard (2) A portable motor that attaches (usually) to the *stern* of a boat

P

Painter A *line* tied to the bow of a *dinghy* used to *moor* it or (sometimes) tow it

Pendant A short length of rope or wire used as a connector, e.g., *mooring pendant* (pronounced pennant)

Pinch To sail too close to the wind, so that the sails *luff*

Pitchpole To *capsize i*n the direction *stern* over *bow*

Point of sail The direction a boat is sailing relative to the wind

Port (1) A harbor

Port (2) The left-hand side of a boat when facing *forward*

Port tack Any course where the wind is blowing on the *port* side of the boat

Preventer A line that prevents the *boom* from crossing the boat in an accidental *jibe*

Prop walk The effect of a *propeller* that pushes the boat's *stern* sideways

Prop wash The flow of water off a turning *propeller*

Propeller A device with radial blades that when rotated deflects water or air to create thrust

Propeller shaft The shaft on which a *propeller* is fitted

Pulpit A guardrail at the *bow* or *stern* of a boat to which (usually) the *lifelines* are connected

R

Ramp A solid walkway along the centerline between the *bridgedeck* and the forward *crossbeam* (also catwalk)

Range Two objects in alignment that provide guidance, as when negotiating a channel, e.g.

Raw water Water drawn from outside the boat

Reach Any *point of sail* between *close-hauled* and a *run*

Reef To reduce the area of a sail that is exposed to the wind

Rig (1) To attach, as a sail

Rig (2) The total assembly of sails, *spars*, and *rigging* aboard a sailboat

Rigging Wires and *lines* used to support *spars* and to control sails

Roach The area toward the *leech* of a sail that extends outside of a straight line between *head* and *clew*

Rode The *line* and/or chain that connects an *anchor* to the boat

Roller furling A mechanism for *furling* a sail by rolling it around its *stay*

Rope To a sailor, raw material for making up *lines*

Rope clutch A device that secures a *line* by clamping onto it

Rudder The movable appendage attached to a boat under the water and with which it can be steered

Rudder stock The shaft that forms the backbone of a *rudder*

Run The *point of sail* on which the wind is *aft*

Running gear The components of the *drive train* after the *shaft coupling*

Running rigging The adjustable *rigging* used to raise and lower or *trim* the sails

S

Safety harness A harness worn around the upper body to which a *safety tether* can be attached

Safety tether A length of strong *line* or webbing with a closable hook at each end

Sailcover A fabric cover for a sail

Saildrive A vertical drive leg that transmits engine power to the propeller

Sail plan The arrangement of sails on a sailboat's *rig*

Sailing by the lee Sailing on a *run* with the wind on the same side of the boat as the *mainsail*

Saloon The area in the *accommodations* used for dining and lounging

Scope The ratio of the length of *anchor rode* deployed to the vertical distance from the boat's *bow* to the *bottom*

Sea breeze A wind that blows from the sea toward the land as a result of hot air rising off the land

Seacock A marine valve, often fitted to a through-hull fitting

Secure To *make fast* (as a *line*)

Seagull striker A braced strut above the forward crossbeam on a catamaran

Shackle A closable metal connector used in *rigging*

Shaft seal A waterproofing seal around the *propeller shaft*

Sheet A *line* used to control the alignment of a sail relative to the boat and the wind

Shorepower Electricity obtained on board through a connection to shoreside power

Shroud A wire that provides *athwartships* support to the *mast*

Sidedeck The *deck* between the *trunk cabin* and the *gunwale*

Slip A *berth* where a boat *docks* between *piers*, *pontoons*, or *pilings*

Snatch block A *block* that opens to fit around the middle of a *line*

Snub To hold a *line* under tension by wrapping it around a *cleat* or a *winch*

Spreader An *athwartships* strut on a *mast* that holds a *shroud* away from the *mast*

Square-top mainsail A *mainsail* with a square top that projects aft of the *mast*

Stanchion A metal post that supports *lifelines*

Standing rigging *Rigging*, e.g. *shrouds* and *stays*, that supports *spars* and that remains in place permanently

Starboard tack Any *course* where the wind is blowing on the *starboard* side of the boat

Stay A piece of *standing rigging* that supports a *mast* in the *fore-and-aft* direction

Staysail A sail set on a *stay* other than the headstay

Steering quadrant A lever in the shape of a quarter circle attached to the *rudder stock* by which the steering cables turn the *rudder*

Stem The very bow of a boat where the *hull* sides meet

Stern The *aft* part of a boat

Stow To put away in a seamanlike manner

Surge To *ease* a loaded line while *snubbing* it to keep it under control

Swinging room The area around which a boat will swing at the full extent of its *anchor rode*

T

Tack (1) The *forward* lower corner of a sail

Tack (2) To change *course* by turning the *bow* of the boat through the wind

Tack (3) A *course* designation according to the side of the boat onto which the wind is blowing (*port* or *starboard*)

Tackle A *line* reeved through a series of *blocks* to gain mechanical advantage

Tail The end of a *working line* (e.g. *halyard*, *sheet*) after the *winch* or *snubber* that is taking the load

Telltale A short length of light yarn or similar material attached to a sail to indicate the flow of air across it and thus the state of the sail's *trim*

Through-hull fitting A fitting in the *hull* used to draw in or discharge water

Tiller A lever used to control the angle of the *rudder* and thereby steer the boat

Toerail A rail fitted around the outside edge of the *deck*

Topping lift A *line* or wire that supports a *boom* when it is not being supported by its sail

Trampoline A taut net strung between the *hulls* of a *multihull*

Transom The more or less flat surface that closes the *hull* at the *stern*

Traveler A car-and-track system that

allows the *mainsheet*'s attachment point to the *deck* to be moved *athwartships*

Trim (1) To adjust a sail by hauling in on the *sheet*

Trim (2) The position a sail is set relative to the wind

Trimaran A *vessel* with three *hulls*

Tripod rig Standing rigging made up of a *forestay* and *shrouds* that support the *mast* without the need for a *backstay*

True wind The wind as observed at a stationary point

Twin screws Two *propellers* installed one on each side of a boat's centerline

Twist In a sail, the difference between the angle of attack at the *foot* and at the *head*

U

Upwind In the direction from which the wind is blowing

V

Vang A piece of *running rigging* used to restrain a *spar*, e.g. *boom vang*

Vented loop A loop of plumbing raised above a boat's *waterline* with a vent to prevent back-siphoning

W

Waterline The line around the *hull* at the surface of the water

Weather helm The tendency of a boat when sailing to *head up* into the wind

Winch A device consisting of a gear-driven drum that provides mechanical advantage when hauling on a *line*; also used to *snub* a line

Windage The surface a boat's *hull*, *rig*, and superstructure present to the wind

Windward Toward the wind

Windward side The side upon which the wind is blowing

Windlass A *winch* used primarily for raising an *anchor*

Wing on wing Sailing on a *run* with the *jib* and *mainsail* set on opposite sides of the boat

Working Of a *sheet*, the one that is currently being used to *trim* the sail

INDEX

Bold entries show illustrations or diagrams.

ANSWERS TO REVIEW QUESTIONS

CATAMARAN EVOLUTION AND ESSENTIALS
page 40-41 answers

1 shrouds, backstay
2 nacelle
3 daggerboard, windward
4 stability, evenly
5 seagull striker
6 crossbeam, aft
7 fully-battened
8 rudders, heeling
9 engines, running gear, cooling, exhaust, electrical, fuel, bilge pumps.
10 start, alternator
11 freshwater, fuel
12 precautions, scalds
13 d   Seagull striker
   b   Ramp/catwalk
   g   Trampoline
   f   Bridgedeck
   a   Forward crossbeam
   c   Deckhouse
   e   Keel
14 i   Diamond stays
   k   Spreader or strut
   l   Mainsheet traveler
   h   Forestay
   j   Topping lift

SAILING, UNDER POWER, SEAMANSHIP
page 80-81 answers

1 2:1 purchase
2 windage, leeway, wider, faster
3 traveler, mainsheet
4 tacking, backed
5 steadily, jib, speed, mainsail
6 boat speed, apparent
7 lowered, retracted (raised)
8 slalom
9 slowly, mainsail
10 wind speeds, sea
11 head up, bear away
12 twin
13 differential, hull
14 keels, windage
15 fuel
16 wheel, engines
17 Close the fuel tank vent, remove loose gear, position dinghy under davits, lower hoisting lines, attach shackles to lifting points, remove drain plug, exit dinghy, raise bow and stern simultaneously, cleat off the tackle, secure with bow and stern lines, check for chafe points
18 transom, points of contact
19 bridle, upwind
20 hand signals
21 bridle
22 jacklines, tethers
23 higher speeds, lack of windward performance, pronounced leeway, helm visibility, high freeboard, propellers close to surface
24 overpowered
25 make a head count, check for injuries, secure crew to inverted boat, secure ditch bag and life raft, salvage whatever you can, send distress signals

Photo credits

All photography by Billy Black except:

Nicolas Claris/Lagoon Catamarans: jacket front, p 16 (right), p 18 (lower), p 21 (upper), p 22; p 28 (lower); Jacques Vapillon: p 8; Herreshoff Marine Museum: p 12; Philipp Hympendahl/James Wharram Designs: p 13; Hobie Cat Company: p 14; Sharon Green/Ultimate Sailing: p 15 (2); Outremer Yachting: p 19 (lower); Fountaine-Pajot Catamarans: p 28 (upper), p 37, p 78; Kinetic Sailing: p 28 (lower left), p 31 (bottom), p 32 (left), p 45 (top, 2), p 73; Seawind Catamarans/Craig Greenhill, Saltwater Images: p 32 (right); Jeremy McGeary: p 34 (right); Yacht Shots BVI: p 49 (image of Sunsail 404); Chris Tucker: jacket back